# wed Acres

## MICHAEL F. TWIST

First published in 1996 by Farming Press

Reprinted 2004 by Farming Books and Videos

**ISBN** 1–904871–00–3

A Catalogue Record for this book is available from the British Library

Published by
Farming Books and Videos Ltd.
PO Box 536
Preston PR2 9ZY
United Kingdom
www.farmingbooksandvideos.com

Front Cover photo: Courtesy of University of Reading, Rural History Centre

Cover design by Pigsty Studio
Typeset by Waverley Typesetters, Galashiels
Printed by Cox & Wyman Ltd, Reading

# Contents

*Dedicated to my son-in-law, Don,*
*whose love of the countryside*
*is as great as mine*

# Introduction

IN 1921, when I was aged two, my parents moved from Oxfordshire to Burnham, South Bucks, where I grew up in Pound Cottage on the Burnham Grove Estate, which was managed by my father for Edward Clifton-Brown, a merchant banker.

The estate took its name from the 'big house' – Burnham Grove. When built, during the reign of George III, it was known as Cants Hill. It has been said that it was originally a royal hunting lodge, further that George IV, when Prince of Wales, housed his first mistress, Perdita Robinson, there. This may or may not have been the case, but one thing which is beyond question is that Thomas Gray, around the 1750s, spent long periods there and, almost certainly, wrote 'Elegy Written in a Country Churchyard' whilst staying at the house. Stoke Poges church is less than half an hour's drive in a pony and trap, and two fields adjacent to The Grove were known as Gray's Meadows. I once remember hearing, when we broke for tea whilst haymaking, one of the old hands telling of 'An ole boy, nigh on two 'undred year ago, who 'ould sit up on hill o' a fine dat an' write po'ms – famous 'e were.'

The estate provided an idyllic way of life, for, from a very early age, I had only one ambition, namely to follow in Father's footsteps. Apart from being mad on farming, particularly on dairy cattle, I was totally 'hooked' on all country activities. In addition I bred a variety of rabbits pigeons and bantams, not only as pets, but to show, the surplus to requirements being sold to supplement my pocket-money of one shilling a week. Further, my brother and I had a positive menagerie of both wild and domestic animals including a Dexter heifer, as described in my first book, *The Spacious Days*.

It is said that every cloud has a silver lining and so it proved to be for me. The 'cloud' appeared when I went off to boarding school, aged eight. I was plagued with illness, culminating in rheumatic fever, when I was fourteen. This, serious as it was, heralded 'the silver lining', for it was decided that my school days were over. I was to continue my book learning, for twelve hours a week, with an excellent tutor, the Reverend Barrington-Baker. That would leave me free, or so I thought, to pursue my many interests at my leisure. However, Father had other ideas and decided it provided a great opportunity for me to get in some serious practical experience on the farms before going to university

The estate, as agricultural estates go, was not large some 1500 acres, made up of five farms: Britwell, Lynch Hill, Biddles, Lees and the Home Farm. As this was before the days of intensive mechanised farming, the estate provided work for over forty men and this did not include the twenty people employed in the 'big house' and gardens. At the beginning of the 1930s a farm labourer's wage, as fixed by the County Wages Board, had risen to 38s for a forty-eight-hour week, but most of those employed on the estate received more than this, particularly the key men, like Harry Wadman, the head shepherd, who certainly would have got double the basic wage, a free house and a number of other perquisites. However, even on the minimum wage, a man, his wife and family could maintain a comfortable if not lavish standard of living, but things were going up in price. A one pound loaf of bread had gone up from 1d to 1½d, whilst a two pound one was 3d. The best cuts of beef, such as sirloin, had risen to 1s (5p) per pound, but many others, together with mutton and pork, were considerably less. Beer had crept up to 5d a pint, terrible dissent being caused around 1936, when a pint of best bitter was increased to the unthinkable price of 6d (2½p) and a packet of Players rose to 10½d, although there were several much cheaper brands.

I had helped out on the farms from an early age, being a competent milker by the time I was ten and trusted to operate a hayrake in the hayfield, but that had all been as and when I pleased. Now it was different, as Father decided what I did and when. With very few exceptions I enjoyed every minute. I enjoyed the work and I enjoyed the company, particularly that of some of the older hands, such as Bill Herbert, who had fought in the Zulu War, 'Gunner' Stingmore, a great character and a veteran of the Boer War, but I was never happier than when I was with Bob Hedges. Bob was one of the gamekeepers, a keen and knowledgeable naturalist, who taught me to shoot at the early age of seven.

The working of the estate revolved largely around the Hampshire Down flock and the shoot, the two being very compatible. In addition there were two herds of pigs, Berkshires and Tamworths. At one stage there were two dairy herds (three if one counted the eight to ten Jersey cows kept at the Home Farm to supply milk and cream to The Grove), beef cattle, free-range hens at Lees Farm and wheat as the main cash crop. All barley and oats grown were for home consumption.

My 'free time' wasn't all work, far from it. There was plenty left for bird-watching, pursuing vermin of various kinds, all of which carried a bounty, so greatly enhancing my pocket-money. There was time to take the gun and go in search of rabbits and pigeons, both terrible pests on farms throughout the country, doing millions of pounds worth of damage to crops. I rode a lot too. It was whilst riding in the old forest of Burnham Beeches that I first met Johnny and his wife, Tilly, gypsies, true Romanies. All sorts of tinkers and the like get described as gypsies, but only the Romanies are really gypsies. I stopped to chat and this led to a pleasant and friendly relationship that lasted up to the outbreak of war. From Johnny I learned many things, some perhaps that I shouldn't have, for he was a rogue, but a most knowledgeable and likeable one.

The years between the end of my school days and going to university were ones of discovery and learning. During the same period I got to know Bill and Tom Hanks, who came to the estate, when required, to make sheep hurdles. They were a veritable fountain of information on country matters and, in particular, woodland lore; whilst their skills, passed down from generation to generation, were many and varied. From them I learned about 'straikes', 'mollies' and 'the dance of death'. They were good days – or were they?

Certainly life was slower, more relaxed. The only stress I can ever remember hearing talked about was the tension one put on a corner post when fencing. Crime wasn't anything like as prevalent as it is now, nor as violent. Widespread pollution was yet to rear its ugly head, hedgerows were filled with a vast assortment of wild flowers, where butterflies lived and bred, as yet untroubled by sprays. But then we hadn't penicillin and a host of other life-saving drugs, we hadn't television and we couldn't fly to the other side of the world in a matter of hours. The pros and cons are endless, the memories numerous, but one thing I am positive about – we had time. Time to enjoy the peace and beauty of God's many gifts throughout the countryside, now so many sadly depleted, or lost forever.

# I

# Half-a-dollar

IT was early May and I had a week off from my studies, for my tutor had been called away on urgent family matters. It is something of a misnomer to say 'a week off', for I spent only three hours, four mornings a week, 'book learning' with the Reverend Barrington-Baker, who in that time was able to implant far more than I would have learned in several weeks at school. Also the rest of the day was frequently not free, far from it, for I was detailed by Father to undertake various jobs on the estate, according to what was happening. This particular day I knew I was scheduled and for several days to come, to getting an insight into hurdle making. Back in the 1920s and 1930s and for many many decades before, there was a great demand for hurdles for penning sheep over crops grown especially for them. The Hampshire Down flock maintained on the estate was the centrepiece around which the entire farming operations revolved. On many farms sheep were essential for preserving a reasonable standard of fertility, particularly in the case of chalky land, or the light gravelly soil like most of that on the Burnham Grove estate, where the 'golden hoof' was a must.

In those days there were a sizeable number of men throughout the country who carried out woodland crafts. Not just hurdle making: they made ladders, hay rakes, produced handles for tools such as hoes, spades, forks and, most intricate, the curved twisting scythe handles. Little was wasted by these specialists, who gleaned a living by the sweat of their brow and the use of inherited skills handed down from father to son. Working under primitive but efficient shelters in their woodland surroundings, some took their skills further and, when not involved in making supplies for farmers, would fashion comfortable seats out of beech for Windsor chairs, to sell to the furniture manufacturers. These seats were shaped with an adze, a tool something like an axe with an arched blade, set at right angles to the handle.

Such craftsmen were Bill and Tom Hanks, father and son, who arrived at Britwell Farm nearly every other spring to make a fresh supply of gate hurdles and repair broken ones with willow and ash poles cut from around the estate. If I remember rightly they came from near Chinnor, in those days a small isolated village in the Chiltern Hills. They were very much their own 'masters' and when there was work to do, they arrived when it suited them. They worked hard, for it was all piecework. The going rate at the time was 2s 6d per hurdle. On an average day they would turn out about three dozen – big money, indeed, for that time. They usually worked eleven to twelve hours, six days a week, with only minimal breaks for meals.

The morning I joined the Hankses they were just about ready to start. They had constructed three equilateral triangles of willow (one for me), mounted horizontally on three legs, not necessarily even. Tom explained to me that they were 'cramps'. The rest of their equipment, carefully laid out on a strip of tarpaulin, consisted of a number of saws, axes, drawknives, two braces and bits, chisels, a couple or three hefty mallets and several 'mollies' – splitting irons, sometimes called 'flammers', which I believe was the correct name for this now obsolete tool, 'molly' almost certainly being a colloquialism. In addition there were two rather oversized sawing-horses – each made of a four-inch-thick piece of timber, about seven inches wide and three feet six inches long, with four legs set at an angle so it couldn't tip over.

Both men gave me a warm welcome. They had known me since I first started visiting the farm on a regular basis at the age of five. Tom tossed a thick leather apron to me.

'Better get this around yer middle, for if you haven't got it on and a drawknife slips, you'll gut yourself.' He grinned, 'So the governor wants you to learn how to make hurdles. Well, boys' first job is stripping. Grab hold of a "drawer" and I'll show you how.'

It was obvious that they had been busy cutting the timber into six foot lengths. These were for the 'runners', the six horizontal bars placed about six inches apart and slotted into the 'straikes', the uprights. It is probable that 'straike' is another colloquialism, for I've never been able to find it in a dictionary and never heard anyone, except the Hankses, use it. Tom picked up a length of timber and placed it in one of the 'cramps'. They were about three feet, or a little more, at the front and slightly higher at the back. A piece of wood was inserted over the front bar and tucked underneath at the back. When one bore down with a drawknife to strip off the bark, the further end came up and 'locked' against the back. When one had removed as much bark as possible the pole was reversed and the other end quickly stripped. Bill had started on some shorter lengths, about three feet six inches long, to make the 'straikes'. These were pointed at one end, leaving about six inches below the bottom runner to drive into the ground and some four inches above the top one as a 'tie'. Hurdle making was not an exact science. A rule might be used when cutting the first lengths, after which the prototypes sufficed as a measure.

I quickly set to work stripping off bark. I was quite used to using a drawknife, for, on wet days, I had spent many hours in the estate workshop under the watchful eye of Charlie Davis, the head carpenter, learning the basics of carpentry. Charlie could make anything, from a cabinet with delicately dovetailed joints, to a vast four-wheeled harvest wagon, even down to the wheels. Charlie had a great liking for crab apple from which to fashion the hub of these, although, due to the lack of supplies, he was often forced to use the more conventional elm. It goes without saying that this was well seasoned, for, in those days, no builder or craftsman worth his salt would consider using unseasoned timber. The spokes were invariably oak and the felloes, which are the sections forming the rim of the wheel, were nearly always ash. Unlike hurdle making, wheel wrighting was a most precise technique, each section having to be carefully measured and shaped. The wheel was fitted together on a 'bed', a level square of concrete with a central hole for the hub to drop into. When assembled the joints were so tight that neither nails nor glue was needed to hold them in place.

At this stage 'Old Jay', the estate blacksmith, took over to do the 'banding' – fitting the iron tyre. This, too, was an art, requiring years of experience. Firstly, the circle of iron was meticulously forged, being made very slightly smaller than the circumference of the wheel. It was heated until nearly white hot and then, with special tongs, it was lifted by 'Old Jay' and a helper and fitted over the wheel as it lay on the 'bed'. Being so hot the iron had expanded and with much rapid hammering and levering, it was quickly worked into position, other workers standing by to pour gallons and gallons of water onto the wheel as soon as the blacksmith gave the order. This, of course, was necessary to stop the felloes catching fire. As the metal cooled it contracted back to its original size, so, when cold, the hub, spokes and felloes were held in a vice-like grip, far stronger than any nails or glue could achieve. Tyring used to fascinate and excite me as a small boy, for, as the tyre cooled, there would be a succession of loud bangs and crackling noises coming from the clouds of steam that engulfed the cooling wheel. The general hubbub was not infrequently added to by roars from 'Old Jay' of 'More water, more water, yer b\*\*\*\*\*\*s. Do yer want to burn the b\*\*\*\*y thing?' It was exciting, for it all had to be done at speed. It was also an example of true craftsmanship, now virtually a lost art.

I worked away steadily stripping off bark, to the accompaniment of much cheerful chat from Tom. Bill was more reticent, but, in spite of all his chat, Tom was a hard and methodical worker. Bill Hanks straightened his back. He'd been drilling holes in the 'straikes'. Two were made as close as possible to each other, then squared up with a mallet and chisel to form the mortises to fit the end of the runners into. He consulted a large pocket watch tucked away in his waistcoat pocket, attached for safety to a buttonhole by a leather thong. 'Right, Tom, didn't think my belly 'ould tell I wrong smack on ten-thirty time for "bait".'

Tom, too, straightened up and turned to me. 'Did you bring a bite to eat?'

I shook my head. 'No, I didn't think it necessary . . .'

5

Old Bill cut in. 'Should 'ave, can't work without a drop of fuel in the tank. We'll give you someut.'

He walked over to his old Ford van, the next model after the famous 'T', took out a wicker basket and opened it up. He lifted out two tin 'flasks', not really flasks as we know them today, just cans with a cork stopper and a tin mug on the top, the forerunner of the thermos flask. Bill poured a 'swig o' tea' for me and offered me a sandwich. I gratefully accepted both, for 'stripping' was hard and thirsty work. Tom smiled. 'Hope you like fat? Them's Dad's favourites, really fatty bacon that is, from one of our own pigs.'

I peeked under the top slice of home-made bread, about half an inch thick, to find nearly the same thickness of meat. My heart sank: I couldn't see even a streak of lean and I loathed fat. I hastily tried to hand the sandwich back. 'On second thoughts I'm not really hungry. I'll wait until lunchtime."

Bill shook his head and laughed. 'Don't talk so daft, get it down you. You're not saying you don't enjoy a bit o' fat bacon? It'll do you a power o' good, it'll grease your gut. Go on, take a good bite.'

I didn't want to be thought a sissy and so did as I was bid, filling my mouth, on the principle that if one had to take something nasty, the sooner one got on with it the sooner the ordeal would be over. Thankfully I was saved the horror of a second mouthful by Harry Wadman, the head shepherd, as he came up the yard to see how the hurdle making was progressing. He was accompanied by two of his Old English Sheepdogs, in those days regularly worked with sheep; both were good friends of mine. Hankses, father and son, turned to greet Harry; the dogs came straight to me. When Bill and Tom again looked in my direction I was rubbing my hands together, ostensibly to remove the crumbs, as I remarked. 'Yes, that was good. Just what I needed to see me through to lunch.' The two dogs stood licking their lips, looking hopefully up at me!

'Have another?'

I shook my head. 'No thanks, Bill, that'll do me nicely. The next day I brought my own 'bait'.

I spent four days with the Hankses, who were excellent company and a fund of information on woodland life. Bill told me how, as a boy, he'd left school at the age of twelve to go to work in the woods with his father and grandfather. Nothing, he assured me, was wasted in those days. For example, offcuts of timber were fashioned into tent pegs, for they were in great demand, particularly from the army. Other short pieces were made into the tines for hayrakes. Birch twigs were 'faggoted' and sold for vinegar refining, the 'brush' being spread in the bottom of vats to help clarify the fermenting brew. Another use for birch twigs was for making besoms or brooms, much used in those days for sweeping up leaves in gardens and suchlike jobs and also, of course, as the accepted conveyance for witches, as depicted in children's books of the time.

Bill told me that when he went to work, his grandfather had a pigsty in an oak wood some three to four miles from their home, where he always fattened a couple of hogs. During the acorn season the pigs would be tethered with a length of rope around a hind leg to a tree to scavenge for acorns an excellent pig food he assured me, better than any grain. Nearly every day the pigs would be moved under another oak and if the men, which included Bill, were working elsewhere then his mother would trudge to the wood and move the pigs. She would frequently carry a couple of buckets of potato peelings, or anything else suitable for feeding the pigs. Bill said he remembered his mother had a little jingle that she was always repeating, which went as follows:

Dearly beloved brethren isn't it a sin,
To peel potatoes and throw away the skin.
For the skin feeds the pigs and the pigs feed you,
Dearly beloved brethren isn't that true?

Pig killing, Bill assured me, was a major local event. The wretched creature would be driven back to the house from the wood, where several neighbours would be waiting to help. When the time was right, two of these would grab the pig and virtually sit it on its bottom on the stone slabs outside the backdoor. His grandfather would then 'stick' it with a long sharp knife, severing the jugular. Seconds after this a bucket would be in place to catch the blood, which was much sought after for making black puddings. Nothing was wasted, even the small intestine, the chitterlings, being carefully preserved and washed to use as sausage skins. The stomach, Bill said, was his grandfather's special perquisite, for he loved it when thoroughly washed, fried and served with onions – tripe and onions.

On pig killing days the big copper in the outhouse would be filled with water from the pump, the fire lit under it, often before dawn, so there was a good supply of boiling water to 'scald' the pig as soon as it was dead, when the bristles could be scraped quickly away. Apparently the cottage had a 'chimley' (Bill didn't seem able to say chimney) which a man could stand up in and in which the hams, often forty-five pounds or more in weight, together with the sides of bacon, would be hung up to be smoked. The only fuel used was wood and when 'smoking' was taking place this was always oak.

I asked Bill if he really still kept a pig for the house.

'Course I do. Where do you think I'd get a decent bit o' fat bacon from otherwise? But we have a sty now, down the bottom of the garden an' buy a bag or two o' meal for 'em, but in the autumn, I still take the hogs to the oak wood. Nothing like acorns for fattening pigs,' he laughed, 'unless it's tatty peelings.'

It was the Hankses who gave me the answer to something that had been puzzling me for some weeks. One day in early April I was sitting on the steps of the keeper's hut in Cocksherd Wood, one of the main coverts, waiting for Bob Hedges, the beat-keeper, a great friend of mine. Two stoats appeared almost simultaneously on the main ride in front of me and started rolling and dancing around in a most extraordinary manner. I couldn't make out what they were up to. At first I thought it was some form of mating ritual, but they seemed to be totally ignoring one another. They must have been aware of my presence, but took no notice. They hadn't been performing for many minutes when a talkative blackbird landed on the ride only feet away from them. The stoats continued their antics, seemingly oblivious of the chattering bird, which was quickly joined by a pair of greenfinches.

What would have happened next I was left to wonder over. for Bob Hedges came around the corner of the ride. His gun leapt to his shoulder as he saw the stoats, but when he realised I was directly in the line of fire, he lowered it and the stoats hurried off unscathed. I told Bill and Tom about this and asked them if they'd ever seen anything like it. Bill replied, 'Oh aye, several times. What you saw were the start of the "dance o' death". Stoats'll fool around in a small open area an', it seems, this'll mesmerise the birds. They be inquisitive little beggars an' get closer an' closer to see what the stoats be up to, then – bang, the stoats'll each nail a bird. I'm tellin' you them's quick, like a striking snake. Once saw an old cock pheasant get too nosy and Mr Stoat had him by the neck in a flash. The cock he didn't think much o' this an' flew up, high as a big oak he went, the stoat still hanging on. Then down crashes the pheasant, knocking his attacker dear, but, quicker nearly than the eye could see, the stoat were back an' buried his teeth in the pheasant's neck. That were it. As soon as the pheasant stopped flapping I ran forward, the stoat ran off an' it were me not Mr Stoat what had pheasant for tea.'

Years later I met a retired gamekeeper who had witnessed the 'dance of death' on several occasions and had even witnessed a similar incident involving a pheasant.

The fourth morning I joined the Hanks, Bill greeted me with, 'This is it, then. Today you make a hurdle right from scratch.'

'Great.' I went to pick up some runners, but was quickly stopped.

'No, no. I said from scratch. Pick your timber, cut it, strip it, split it, the lot.

'You think I can't.'

'Time'll tell, time'll tell.'

All went well until I got hold of a 'molly' and tried to split the lengths of willow I'd chosen. It looked so simple when Tom or Bill did it, but I messed up several pieces before I had the five runners, two 'straikes' and the 'strengtherners', a centre upright and two diagonal supports that ran from the top of the latter to the bottom 'runner' where they were mortised into the 'straike'. At last I was ready to assemble my hurdle. I whacked in the nails and stood up as I admired my handiwork.

'There you are. How about that?'

Bill and Tom examined the hurdle without saying a word, then Bill nodded his head. 'Not bad not bad at all. 'Only one thing wrong.' I was disappointed by this last remark. I thought it was an excellent hurdle, just as good as any of the ones the Hankses had made, well, nearly as good.

'What?'

Bill pulled out his watch. 'What's wrong? I'll tell you what's wrong, the time. Took you two hours and about twenty-three minutes to make one b****y hurdle. At half-a-dollar a time you wouldn't get very fat at that rate.'

He paused, felt in the pocket of his well-worn corduroy trousers and pulled out a half-crown and tossed it to me. 'There you are, that's the going rate. Reckon that's the first and last money you'll ever earn making hurdles. Keep it as a memento.'

I did, and, somewhere, I still have it to this day. Not only is it a reminder of the one and only hurdle I ever made, but it is a reminder of the days when crown pieces, large five shilling coins, could still be obtained through the bank and the exchange rate was four dollars to the pound, hence the tag half-a-dollar for a half-crown.

# 2

# *What's in a Name?*

❧

THERE was one thing I could be certain of back in the 1930s: that my life would never be boring or become repetitive. I arrived home one lunchtime in mid June, from my morning studies, to be told by Father that one of the herdsmen at Lynch Hill Farm had been rushed to hospital with appendicitis. This was followed only a couple of hours later by another member of the dairy staff having a flaming row with Jim Light, the head herdsman, before walking out. So instead of there being four men, to do the afternoon milking, there were only two.

Machine milking was still much in its infancy and viewed with considerable suspicion by the majority of dairy farmers, many of whom decried it as being 'not nartural'. Father was a fringe member of this sect, but not due to the fact that it wasn't natural, but because many farmers who had installed machines claimed it brought about far more incidents of mastitis than hand milking. This theory was strongly supported by Aubrey Ward, the veterinary surgeon who did the work for the estate. So, although we had one of the most modern cowsheds in the country, milking at Lynch Hill was still done by hand.

I listened to Father, then asked, 'What are you going to do?'

He smiled. 'Well, to start with, you can fill one vacancy.' This pleased me greatly, for I had gained my 'Clean Milker's Certificate' a couple of years previously.

Cleanliness was the key to the production of 'Grade A' milk. This entailed the scrupulous grooming of the cows, washing and drying the udders before starting milking, plus drawing off the foremilk to check for mastitis. Milking had to be done dry-handed and into dome-topped pails. The pail tops were to help stop any foreign bodies from falling into the milk, thus improving its cleanliness and so its keeping quality, for the time about which I write was well before pasteurisation. In those days, at least in small country towns and villages, the milkman came around with a horse-drawn float, with several large churns, most of which were fitted with taps, and drew off what the housewives required into a pint measure. If the churn did not have a tap (and a number hadn't), then he'd just ladle the milk out from the top of the churn and pour it into the customer's jug. If the housewife was going out, she'd leave a jug with a note on the doorstep. I can remember that this was a common sight in and around Burnham, particularly in the 1920s.

I mentioned dry-hand milking. I can still vividly recall seeing old Murkett, the cowman who looked after the small Jersey herd kept to supply milk to the 'big house', settle down on his milking-stool by a cow, clear the mucus from his nose with his fingers, spit on his hands and start milking. Alternatively, he and others of his generation would give a good squirt of milk to each hand before starting, claiming that 'it were more "nartural", more like a calf a suckin'. However, such practices were taboo in the production of 'Grade A' milk, and the reason that County Councils throughout the country brought in a scheme whereby milkers could take an exam and obtain a 'Clean Milker's Certificate'. In the early days of the 'Grade A' scheme the requirements to produce such milk were looked upon as a bit of a joke and led to an imaginary conversation between a farmer and his herdsman in the magazine *Dairy Farmer* that went something like this:

FARMER: 'Ready for milking, Bill?'

HERDSMAN: 'Yes, boss.'

FARMER: 'Are you sure? Have you dusted the cowshed, bathed the cows, sterilised their udders and boiled your hands?'

HERDSMAN: 'Yes, boss.'

FARMER: 'Right, then you can set the barn on fire and start milking.'

I remember this amused Father greatly and he cut it out, had it mounted, framed and hung in the Lynch Hill cowshed, together with a rider which read, 'Get as close to this as you can, but *don't* burn down the barn.' It could well have supplied part of the inspiration that led to Lynch Hill winning the Gold Cup for producing the cleanest milk in the county for a number of years in succession.

I did my afternoon stint and told Jim Light that I'd see him at 5.00 a.m. the following morning, by which time the cows would have been brought in from the fields, groomed and it would be time to start milking. I climbed out of my bed just before 4.30 a.m., quickly dressed, collected my bike from the garage and started out along the lane in the direction of the farm. It was a gorgeous summer morning, the dew still sparkling in the early sunlight and the birds singing; in fact, life was good.

As I crossed the main road, itself little more than a lane, into the one leading to Lynch Hill, I spotted Bob Hedges in Pump Meadow, away to my left, checking his snares in the never-ending war against rabbits. I raced down the hill towards Lammas Wood to get up speed for the stiff climb up Lynch Hill. As a lad I had always assumed that in the dark and not-so-distant past, someone had been 'strung up' on the big oak tree to the right of the hill for some egregious crime such as sheep stealing, but when I started helping in the hay and harvest field, I learned that some of the older farm labourers had a different idea as to how the hill came by its name. Three in particular used to love telling the tale when there was a break for tea – Jack Adaway, 'Gunner' Stingmore and Bill Herbert. The meat of the story remained the same; it was just the detail that varied according to who had the floor and the amount of time available.

According to all three, sometime towards the end of the seventeenth century, or early in the eighteenth, a certain Jack Lynch became so angered by his wife's continued infidelity that he decided to publicly show his displeasure and shame her before all and sundry. That he was going to do this became widely known and, on the appointed day, a large crowd gathered at the foot of the hill. The aggrieved husband arrived with his wife in a horse and cart. At the foot of the hill he stopped, dragged her out, tied her wrists to the back of the cart, stripped her to the waist and then drove the horse slowly to the top of the hill while lambasting her back with a stout hazel switch. In old Bill Herbert's telling he always said, "T was done wit' parson's blessin'." 'Gunner' always added that every time the switch cut into the back of the unfortunate woman, Lynch cried out, 'Praise the Lord'. Fact or fiction? There is no way of finding out, but certainly the story had been passed down through three different families. One of the old hands, who worked on the estate, as he made his way back from the harvest field one evening, caught his granddaughter 'being a naughty little girl' with her boyfriend under a hedge. He told his workmates he thrashed the lad and threatened to take the lass up Lynch Hill if she ever did anything so sinful again before she was married, or, at least, he said, he'd give her a taste of what Jack Lynch was reputed to have given his wife. Obviously the girl believed him, for she became the model of propriety. How things have changed in sixty years!

I milked ten cows that morning and for those who haven't tried it, however competent you are, I can assure them that it is hard work, particularly if one is not doing it regularly. The strain on the muscles in the wrist and arms can be tremendous. It was 8.15 a.m. when I entered my home, to be greeted by Mother. 'You're late. You know that breakfast is at eight o'clock sharp. Get yourself washed. Your breakfast is on top of the stove.'

Breakfast was always a good fry-up: eggs, bacon, sausages, fried potatoes and, often, in the late summer and autumn, mushrooms that had been growing in the fields less than an hour earlier. This was followed by toast, home-made butter and marmalade, or honey from the hives situated in the field just beyond the garden fence. Virtually everything that could be was home produced. On thinking back, it was quite amazing what Mother achieved, when comparing a modern kitchen with the appliances and facilities which were available to her: a four-burner Valor oil stove, with a removable oven which could be placed over any two of the burners when required, and a north-facing larder with a meat-safe. The latter, for those not familiar with this important necessity of the 1930s and earlier, was like a cupboard with open sides covered with wire gauze. This kept the flies and other insects out and allowed the air to circulate around the contents. Actually, compared with the majority of houses early in the 1930s, we were very modern and well equipped, for Father had purchased a large, almost brand-new, domestic refrigerator at a farm sale for £5. It did noble service for more than forty years, as, in those days, things were built to last.

As I have said, everything, when possible, was home-made or home-grown. Every summer Mother made around fifty pounds of strawberry jam and a similar amount of raspberry, as well as cherry, plum and gooseberry, along with an adequate supply of redcurrant jelly. As soon as the Seville oranges were available, she would set to and make pounds and pounds of marmalade, until her store cupboards were full. Every day a large pan of milk would be scalded, that is brought gently to the boil, and then allowed to cool. The cream would rise and, when skimmed off, one had delicious clotted cream, much like old-fashioned Devonshire farmhouse cream. Mother made butter about twice a week in a glass screw-topped churn. She nearly always added a half-crown, or florin, first carefully sterilised in boiling water, before being liberally coated with butter and dropped into the cream. This, she claimed, always made the butter form more quickly; certainly churning never took her long. The cakes she baked in her tin oven on the Valor stove were noted, particularly throughout much of the pedigree livestock world, and world really meant just that, for buyers came from all corners of the globe to buy livestock from the Burnham Grove Estate, mainly Berkshire and Tamworth pigs, Hampshire Down sheep and the occasional Red Poll cow or young bull – all, sadly, with the possible exception of the Hamps, now classified as rare breeds.

There is no doubt we fed well and, on reflection, I marvel at what my parents achieved. Father told me, years later, that when he took over the management of the estate he received £5 per week, a rent and rates-free house, fuel, transport, milk, eggs and all the help he needed in the garden. After two years his salary went up to £425 per annum and remained the same for at least a decade, before reaching £650 a year, just before the Second World War, which was about the same as a Member of Parliament received at that time. In those days one never heard about inflation, and certainly, even if it existed, which I suppose it must have to a very small degree, wages and salaries were not geared to it and increases in pay were purely due to results. If you had a good job, as Father had, one was satisfied and gave of one's best. As far as being paid for helping out with the milking, the thought never entered my head. Actually, in the past I had tried to get paid for doing various jobs on the estate, but was quickly told that I was lucky to have the opportunity to learn and that there were two pupils (potential farmers or managers) paying to have the chance of doing what I did. The only way I had of earning money on the farm was flat-hoeing and thinning root crops, all of which was done as piecework.

Milking was no hardship, for dairy cattle were my special interest. One of the highlights of my year, if not *the* highlight, was visiting the Dairy Show held at Olympia in London. This had become an annual event long before I had finished at school, for Father claimed that what I learned there would be of far more use to me than Latin verbs or algebra. An added bonus held in conjunction with it was the National Poultry Show, which included pigeons and bantams, the breeding and showing of both being one of my major pastimes. It was at the Dairy Show in the late 1920s or early 1930s that I discovered the magazine, *Dairy Farmer* when going round the trade stands. The moment I skimmed through a copy I was hooked; I simply had to have it on a regular basis and pleaded with Father to let me. He agreed, but only if I gave up one of my two weekly comics, to which I readily agreed. Ironically one of the first copies I received contained a limerick which got me into trouble and which I can remember to this day. It went as follows:

> There was a young fellow called Starkie,
> Who had an affair with a darkie,
> The result of his sins
> Was quadruplets, not twins,
> One white, one black and two khaki.

In my innocence – for sex wasn't something with which we were brainwashed as children are today via television and, indeed, in school – I thought 'affair' meant fight. At the preparatory school I attended we took it in turns to sit next to the headmaster at lunch, the object of the exercise being that we had to make intelligent conversation. When next my turn came, I immediately started on my favourite subject, dairy farming, and told him about this wonderful new magazine. Then, naively, I recited my recently learned limerick. The result was stunning: there was absolute silence before the Head, in thunderous tones, ordered me to leave the table and wait outside his study. Having stood, shaking at the knees for about twenty minutes, I was taken into the holy of holies and verbally castigated and threatened with the cane for reciting a vulgar and obscene limerick! However, whilst I was puzzled as to what I had done wrong, it in no way lessened my enjoyment of *Dairy Farmer*. Actually it taught me to keep my mouth shut and never to repeat anything unless I was sure exactly what it meant.

# 3
# Of Hares and Hedgehogs

THE advent of spring, that exciting period when the countryside comes to life, filled the days to capacity There was always so much to do, so much to watch and in those days, there was time to do it, for the rhythm of life was not geared to obsessions for sitcoms on television or serials on the radio. Life, at least in the country, whilst often hard, was for living, enjoying God's gifts and the wonders of nature. I can never remember children, or adults, being bored; everyone whom

I knew had an interest. It might have been gardening, peaceful walks in the countryside, possibly bird watching or collecting wild flowers for pressing, fishing or, if of a felonious disposition, a little surreptitious poaching of the unwary rabbit. High in the recreational pastimes came 'The Fancy' – the breeding and showing of many varieties of domestic rabbits, poultry and pigeons.

I would watch anxiously for the first signs that winter was coming to an end, like rooks gathering twigs with which to refurbish their nests and bluebells pushing up shoots through a carpet of leaves in the woods. Mad March hares (although they often started their antics in February) would begin boxing, kicking, jumping as the bucks fought among themselves over a doe, or sometimes the displaying would be between a doe and several bucks, the former not being ready to receive the attentions of a mate. I would watch them for hours, usually from The Belt which bisected Big Field. One afternoon, with Bob Hedges, I watched nine hares performing their 'ballet', their grunts and hisses quite audible as they circled around one another. It was a long show, a good twenty minutes before the 'cast' was reduced to two, a buck and a doe, but, the sparring continued until suddenly it ceased and they mated. That afternoon was the only time I actually saw hares mate. The buck, satiated, loped off, whilst the doe remained crouched low to the ground. Suddenly she set off at speed towards the nearest of her previous wooers. After a brief preliminary courtship she mated again.

The buck departed, quickly to be replaced by another, that had been hovering in the background. However, it seemed the doe had had enough, for after sparring for a couple of minutes she hightailed it, hotly pursued by her new suitor, across the field and disappeared through the hedge into Deep Lane.

Bob and I had watched, well hidden, from behind a bush, fortunately downwind from where they cavorted. Had this not been the case they would have departed, for hares have a keen sense of smell and, indeed, hearing, although it is questionable whether their sight is equally attuned, at least when looking straight ahead.

A family of gypsies, true Romanies, clean proud people used to pass regularly through the district. Their three horse-drawn caravans were both picturesque and spotless and their horses and dogs well cared for, as were two Old English gamecocks that would strut around their camp. Sometimes they would camp on the edge of the road, or, quite contrary to by-laws, in Burnham Beeches. Unlike the hippie-type so-called 'travellers' of today, they did not leave filth and rubbish behind them, desecrating the countryside. Many times, when riding in The Beeches, I would come across them and stop for a chat.

I was particularly attracted to three brindle lurchers with the group. They epitomised the poem, 'The New Anubis', written by my father's good friend, Patrick Chalmers, a well-known author and poet back in the 1930s. The poem went as follows:

All along the moorland road a caravan there comes
Where the piping curlew whistle and the brown snipe drums;
    And a long lean dog
    At a sling jig-jog,
A poacher to the eyelids as all the lurcher clan
Follows silent as a shadow and as clever as a man.

His master on the splashboard, oh, of ancient race he is;
He came down out of Egypt, as did all the Romanys:
    With a hard hawk face
    Of an old king race,
His hair is black and snaky and his cheek as brown as tea
And pyramids and poaching-dogs are made by such as he.

Now, the dog he looks as solemn as a beak upon the bench.
But he'll pounce and pick a hare up, and he'll kill her with
a wrench,
  Or he'll sneak around a rick
  And bring back a turkey chick
And you'll wonder how they got him all his cockaleerie
fakes;
Well, his master comes of people who turn walking-sticks
to snakes.
There was once a God in Egypt, when gods they first
began,
With the muzzle of a lurcher on the body of man:
  But the Pharoah of today
  He has changed the ancient way,
And has found him a familiar by his caravan to jog,
With the headpiece of a Solomon, the body of a dog.

One couple that I was particularly friendly with was Johnny
(who owned the lurchers) and his wife, Tilly. I always felt
slightly guilty, for it was like fraternising with the enemy. I
knew that with as little thought as he would give to drinking
a cup of tea, Johnny would set a snare along a hedgerow for
an unsuspecting hare or rabbit, or knock a pheasant off its
roost with a well-aimed shot from his catapult. Johnny was
the indisputable leader of the group, although frequently he
preferred to travel alone with Tilly. He was of medium stature,
dark, wiry, with a nose that gave his features a raptorial look. He
had a great sense of humour, even if at times it was somewhat
bizarre. His great delight was to bait the police, particularly PC
Brewer, who used to patrol from Farnham Common down to
Farnham Royal, part of The Beeches and East Burnham, which
took him to the western boundary of Big Field. He was known
locally as 'Ole Five Minutes', for if there was any crime on his
patch, be it poaching or housebreaking, he invariably said, 'If

I'd been five minutes earlier, I'd have caught them red-handed.'
He seldom ever took a case to court, but trundling around on
his bike, he was a restraining influence on those whose thoughts
might turn towards the perpetration of a little petty larceny.
Strangely, he seemed to swallow 'hook, line and sinker' any tale
Johnny might concoct.

It was Johnny who told me that hares had poor sight when
looking straight ahead and went on to tell me how to catch a
hare without the aid of a net, dog or snare, just with one's bare
hands. According to my informant, having first spotted a hare,
roughly in the middle of a field, you set off to walk the boundary.
At the start of the second lap you drew in towards the quarry by
some ten to fifteen yards and then continued round and round in
ever-decreasing circles. Plenty of time was an important factor,
as it wasn't something that could be rushed. Also, it was most
important to keep going at the same pace and, if one did, the hare
was in the bag, or as Johnny put it, in the pot. He stressed how
important it was to hold the hare's attention one hundred per cent;
any distraction and 'puss' would be off. When one got really close
it was imperative to retain the same even speed, inching in each
circuit, until, finally, one dived onto the hare, but always from
in front. Johnny assured me that from behind one hadn't a hope,
as the hare's reflexes would be too quick, but coming in from the
front, its impaired eyesight gave the 'hunter' that split-second
advantage. He swore he'd taken many a hare by this method and
added, with a wicked grin, that if apprehended by a gamekeeper,
before making the catch, one could claim to be just aimlessly
taking a stroll. Johnny's theory about hares' sight I found verified,
years later, in Bryan Vesey-Fitzgerald's book, *It's My Delight*.

Twice I tried to put Johnny's hare catching technique into
practice. Once, after an hour in Big Field, I seemed to be doing well.
I was within fifteen yards of my quarry, when George Devonshire

another of the gamekeepers, shot a stoat as he walked along the side of The Belt – the mesmeric spell was broken and 'puss' was away. Later the same year I tried again. I spotted a hare just about in the middle of some ten acres of fallow ground, being part of Forty Acres. I started to walk, the circles getting ever smaller, and after well over an hour I was within feet of my intended victim, as she tucked down tight into her form, as still as though she was carved in stone, not even a twitch of a whisker. My heart raced and, undoubtedly, the adrenalin flowed, one more circuit and – woosh, I'd make dive and it would be jugged hare for dinner! Suddenly the peace and quiet of the September afternoon was broken by the thudding of horses' hooves, as my brother, Ralph, accompanied by a friend, galloped their mounts out towards me. The spell was broken and my intended prey was streaking across the field. Seconds, just seconds, was all that had been needed, and I would have had my chance, but at least I was close enough to know that Johnny had not been pulling my leg – it would be possible, subject to no distractions to catch a hare with one's bare hands. However, I was not a happy boy as my brother rode up and my mood was certainly not improved by his calling out, 'Do you realise you nearly walked on a hare?'

Some months later, when out riding in The Beeches, I came across Johnny and his companions camped in one of the remoter parts of the old forest. They were sitting around an inviting log fire having a meal. At Johnny's invitation I dismounted and perched on the end of the old tree trunk on which he and Tilly were sitting. Both had plates of stew, and Johnny held his out to me. 'Try a bit of meat.'

I looked suspiciously at it. 'What is it?'

'Try it. You'll like it.'

Rather warily, I took a piece with my fingers and carefully examined it. It was whitish and in texture something akin to rabbit. I tasted it gingerly. It was good, so I put the remainder in my mouth and chewed away happily. Not that it needed much chewing, for it was very tender and succulent, but I couldn't pinpoint the flavour – a sort of mixture of rabbit, chicken and, possibly, pork.

'Yes, very nice, but what is it?'

'Hedgehog.'

I positively gagged, much to the amusement of my companions. Johnny grinned from ear to ear.

'What's the matter? They're clean-living animals. We consider them a great delicacy.'

I knew that what Johnny had said about them being clean-living animals was true, but whilst my brain agreed my stomach was not convinced. We, or rather Ralph, had a pet hedgehog at home, Mr Hedgepiggy, and the thought that I'd just had a large mouthful of one of his cousins did nothing to improve my feelings. Tilly, who had been laughing so much that the tears were running down her cheeks, joined in the conversation.

'The dogs hunt them out and bring them back at night. Johnny does the necessary, guts them, then I wrap them in clay and bake them in the fire. When they are cooked all the skin and spines come away with the clay and you are left with tender juicy meat. Do you know I've never had a tough one, not like some of the butcher's meat you get.'

Still feeling distinctly queasy, I climbed back onto my horse and prepared to ride away. As I did so one of the gamecocks flew up onto a nearby branch and crowed lustily. They never seemed to go far from the camp and I'd never seen them squaring up to each other, or show any aggression. Curiosity got the better of me.

'Tell me, Johnny, what do you use your cocks for, fighting?'

'Yes and no, but not in the way you think. One day I might tell you. Good luck, nice to see you.' He laughed. 'Next time

Bob Hedges gets a 'hog' in a tunnel-trap, ask him to keep it for you and take it home to your ma to cook.' I felt the bile rising up in my throat and hastily gave my horse a dig in the ribs and rode away.

The gestation period of a hare is about thirty days, and a doe will often produce young twice, sometimes three times, during the breeding season. If the weather has been mild, it's not unusual to find their young, called leverets, at the end of March or early April. The size of a litter varies: it may be as small as two or even the occasional singleton, or may go up to six, although I have read where litters of eight have been recorded. Of all the mammals in these isles, leverets are easily the most appealing and gorgeous young. Unlike rabbits, rats, mice, they are born covered with hair; further, they do not have the disadvantage of the former, or, indeed, fox cubs, baby badgers, stoats – in fact all British wild animals – of being blind at birth. Leverets are born open-eyed and can run from the moment of birth, which usually occurs in the middle of an arable field, exposed to all the elements. Once the litter has been born the doe scratches out a separate form for each of her babies and carries them in her mouth, in the same way that a cat will carry a kitten, to their respective homes. She suckles them in turn, mostly at night, and at four to five weeks they are completely self-determining and no longer in need of their dam.

Hares are classified as game, a tribute not paid to the lowly cony, and were hunted with hounds, by the nobility, long before hunting foxes became fashionable. How far back the tradition of hare hunting extends is hard to say, but it is on record that around 480 to 450 BC, the Greek soldier and historian, Xenophon, a friend of Socrates, hunted hares with hounds that followed their quarry by scent, not sight as do greyhounds.

During the course of my life I have, on a number of occasions, seen hares on various beaches and wondered at their presence. It was only a few years ago that I learned the reason. They are, of course, vegetarians and can inflict a great deal of damage to farm crops, but they also have a great yen for certain plants whose habitat is the foreshaw. Favourite amongst these, according to Charles Cornish, a naturalist of some note in the early part of the century, is the sea-pea (*Lathyrus maritima*), and he claims to have seen hares swim wide estuaries to reach supplies of this much-sought-after 'hare delicacy'.

For many hundreds of years a certain mystique has built up around hares, for they are the centre of many fables, from turning into witches to changing sex, and in some of the oldest Welsh laws it is stated that 'The hare is outside legal valuation, since in one month it is a female and in the next a male.' Truly, then, a magical animal, but to me it remains one of grace, power and, when young, of unequalled beauty.

# 4
# *Pride*

WHEN out walking recently I watched a vast multi-furrowed reversible plough and an equally vast tractor turning over more land in an hour than we could have done in a day sixty years ago, when much of the ploughing was still done with horses. As I stood looking I realised something was wrong, and suddenly it dawned on me what it was: there were no birds following the plough. My thoughts drifted back to my first full day ploughing with a tractor. It was late in February, at a guess 1934, for I know I was receiving tuition from the Rev

Barrington-Baker and, during that time, Fridays were free. Tom Brookling, one of the two tractor drivers on the estate, was off sick, and due to the terrible weather we'd been having, the ploughing was very behind schedule. In addition to the regular carters, there were plenty of men on the farm staff who could plough with horses, but none of these could drive a tractor. I, on the other hand, had been doing so since the age of ten or eleven, under the watchful eye of Tom, or Jack Keen, the head tractor driver. Hearing of the former's illness I eagerly volunteered, for I found ploughing a most rewarding and satisfying pastime. Further – and I must admit this was very much to the fore in my mind – I thought I might earn myself a few shillings. After a slight hesitation by Father, my offer was accepted, for I would not be working on my own, since I'd be in the same field as Jack. However, my hopes that I might get paid were quickly dashed. Father briskly told me that boys did not get paid to learn and, anyway, I shouldn't expect to be financially rewarded for helping out in an emergency.

The tractor I would be using was a Fordson, with spade-lug wheels. A reliable, simple machine, costing, if I remember rightly, around £120, that gave little trouble and seldom, if ever, let one down. The only thing I can recollect failing was magnetos. There was no battery, no question of turning a key and the engine starting, one had to 'swing' it with a starting handle – sometimes a hard job on a cold winter's morning – and there could be a hell of a kickback, which could, literally, break the wrist of the unwary. The trick was not to grasp the handle tightly, but hold it so one's thumb and fingers were on the same side. Then, if there was a kick, the handle flew harmlessly out of one's hand. The engine started on petrol and, when warm, it was switched over to TVO (paraffin). It chugged comfortably along with a two-furrow plough and, on a good day, one might hope to turn over three to four acres.

It was not exactly a comfortable mode of transport, for the seat was cast iron, mounted on an angled steel arm, which had a modicum of give in it and so acted, to a very limited extent, as a shock absorber. I suppose it minimally eased the worst of the spine-jarring jolts and bumps, but it was still a pretty rough ride! It was common practice to partially fill an old corn sack with hay, or straw, to make a cushion. No such refinement was supplied by the makers, nor was a cab or windscreen; when tractor driving one was open to the elements. On a wet day it was a case of donning what waterproof clothing one had and carrying on regardless, as it had to be very wet to stop. It was said by some of the men who worked on the land that only when the rain was running out of the seat of their trousers, then and only then, would Tom Rose, the foreman, say it was too wet to carry on working outside.

Friday morning I breakfasted soon after 6.00 a.m. and hurried to Lynch Hill to fill up with fuel, check the oil and make sure the bandings, two heavy half-circles of flat iron, about nine inches wide, that were bolted over the spadelugs on each wheel, were secure. These were to stop damaging the road and, quite literally, ripping it up. All was ready by seven o'clock and I hooked up to a Ransome two-furrow plough, balancing my bike precariously on top of it. Behind the plough was attached a small trailer, covered with an apex roof, made by Charlie Davis and 'Old Jay'. It contained cans of fuel, ploughshares, various bolts, tools and sundry spares that might be needed. We were going to plough Forty Acres at Biddles Farm, a large field for those days. Normally fields were smaller, as the mania for ripping out hedges, creating prairies and destroying the habitat for so much of the wildlife was not yet in vogue.

Jack, whose tractor also pulled a plough and trailer, led off out of the yard. It was still only half light as we made our way along the gravel road, the centre of which was well roughed up by the iron shoes of the horses that regularly traversed it. We trundled along at five to six miles an hour, for banded wheels were not exactly designed for speed! As we turned into Biddles Lane I could just see Harry Stanley, one of the shepherds, shaking out food into long wooden troughs for some fifty wether hoggets, being penned over turnips in part of Big Field, which would be fattened off by the spring and go as prime mutton. In those days mutton, at 9d to 10d a pound, with a good inch to an inch and a half of fat across the loin, was in great demand and preferred by many to lamb, which was frequently said to lack enough fat.

Most of the fatstock on the estate was sold privately to local butchers, the main of these being Arthur Saunders, who apart from owning a lucrative stud-farm in Sussex, had butcher's shops in Taplow, Maidenhead and Windsor, the latter being of particular importance, as it supplied meat to the castle. King George V was, of course, on the throne at that time. Queen Mary, unattended, often visited the local shops when at Windsor. She took a keen interest in the running of the royal households, and it was not unusual for her to inspect the kitchens. One morning when Arthur Saunders was visiting his Windsor branch, in strode the Queen carrying a large wicker shopping basket, which she plonked down on the counter. She then demanded to see Mr Saunders. Arthur made himself known. Her Majesty eyed him up and down, and then imperiously demanded, 'Why are you not wearing an apron?'

'Because, Ma'am, I don't work in my shops.'

Her Majesty's reply was curt and to the point. 'Then you should do, Mr Saunders, you should do. That is, if you wish to retain the patronage of the castle. Now, in future, don't ever send mutton like this again. No fat, no fat at all.' As she said this she took four legs of lamb from her basket, slapped them down on the counter and departed. It transpired that the lamb had been obtained, with some difficulty, following a special order from the Steward of the Household, or whoever dealt with such matters. An hour later the four legs were returned to the castle accompanied by, just to be on the safe side, four nice fat legs of mutton, the latter with the compliments of Arthur Saunders.

I heard him tell the above many times and he swore it was true. Further, that some days later Her Majesty had again called at the shop to say the 'mutton' had been excellent. I don't doubt the story, for the Queen was a frequent visitor to Biggs, the jewellers in Maidenhead, who specialised in antique silver. She would walk in, usually unaccompanied, and just browse. She had told the manager, Mr Leonard, a friend of my parents, that she wished to be ignored and would call him if she required his services.

We arrived at Forty Acres and left our trailers just inside the entrance to the field. Jack, a first-class ploughman and winner of numerous competitions, said he would mark out the field in 'lands', that is, cutting a furrow and then coming back on the opposite side, throwing up a 'ridge'. These would be at intervals of two chains (44 yards) apart, right across the field. After he had one ridge set up I was to start.

As I waited I watched several flocks of fieldfares fly chattering overhead. They have a very distinctive call, sounding something like 'chack-chack-chack' and are mostly winter migrants from the Continent. Back in the 1920s and 1930s they could be seen in hundreds, indeed thousands, over the majority of the country. Frequently mixed with them would be redwings, another of our winter visitors. Sadly, like so much of our wild life, they have become something of a rarity, instead of being part of the normal winter scene. Many of the old country folk claimed fieldfare were excellent eating, in fact quite a delicacy, and were delicious if roasted and served on slices of fried bread.

It wasn't freezing, but although I had plenty of clothes on, it was cold standing about waiting to begin. The sky was heavy and it looked as though snow was a distinct possibility. It was after eight o'clock when I dropped the plough in and started to cut my first furrows. I stopped several times to make minor adjustments to the setting, probably not really necessary, but I knew Jack would be watching as he came back down the field and it gave me a feeling of importance – for it was the first time I had been entrusted to plough unsupervised. It seemed an interminable journey, at about four to five miles an hour, to the big hedge at the far end of the field, but eventually I got there, yanked the cord to trip the plough, pulled out onto the headland, turned and began the long haul back.

Slowly, but surely, the width of ploughed ground increased. Jack had started on the adjoining 'land', having finished marking out the field, diminishing the space between us by some four feet or so every time we passed on the inner leg of our work. By now we were being followed by a host of birds – rooks, starlings, blackheaded gulls, numerous smaller birds such as chaffinches, greenfinches, pied wagtails and, near the hedges at either end of the field, blackbirds, thrushes and the occasional robin – for we were turning up a rare feast of worms, slugs, centipedes, leatherjackets and numerous other sources of food. What always intrigued me was how the rooks, starlings, etcetera knew? I could easily understand about the smaller birds, because the surrounding hedges were their habitat, but as I stood waiting, earlier in the morning, I hadn't seen a rook, starling or gull anywhere in the area. Now there were scores of rooks and gulls following the ploughs and, literally, hundreds of starlings. What sixth sense told them 'dinner was served'? These days one sees few birds following the plough, for apart from their numbers being greatly depleted, turning the soil does not produce the wealth of food it did fifty to sixty years ago. The constant use of chemical fertilisers and pesticides, in various forms, has annihilated so many grubs and organisms once so prolific in the soil.

At as near noon as possible Jack stopped on the headland and settled down under the hedge for his dinner. Almost certainly it consisted of thick slices of crusty bread with cheese, followed by fruit cake and washed down with cold tea. I raced home on my bike, had lunch and tore back to Forty Acres, arriving at about five minutes to one. Although the staff were allowed an hour in the middle of the day, it was clear that Jack had not taken his full quota, for he had obviously already completed one turn of the field since I left him and was again halfway to the far hedge. It was a matter of pride, to all concerned, that everything should be the best, and that included having the ploughing done so that the spring corn could be sown at the optimum time. This would have been uppermost in Jack's mind, taking precedence over his right to have an hour's break.

It was getting dark as I pulled my tractor in on the headland beside Jack's, which he was already sheeting up for the night. Although the tractor garage at Lynch Hill was only a little over a mile away, there was no question of driving back to the farm – it would take far too long to 'band up', hence the trailers and supplies of fuel. When both tractors were covered for the night, Jack asked me if I was coming the next day. I replied that I would be. Normally on a Saturday the staff knocked-off at twelve and I had planned to go pigeon shooting in the afternoon I wasn't too happy therefore when Jack replied 'Good if we stick at it, by this time tomorrow we'll have about a third of the field ploughed, if not more. You done real well today, reckon we'll make a ploughman of you yet. Now you get on home, don't wait for me, it'll only take me ten or twelve minutes to walk back to my place.'

As I rode off flocks of green plover were flying in low over the lane, giving their characteristic call of 'pee-weat, as they descended onto the fresh plough. I stopped at the junction with Deep Lane and watched, as plover continued to swoop in low over the hedge, in flocks of twenty or thirty, their plaintive cry almost continuous.

As I stood watching and listening, another sound became audible, the clop-clop of horses coming along the lane. Minutes later two great Shires loomed up through the rapidly fading light, followed a yard or two behind by another pair. Sitting sideways on one of the first two was Arthur Goodchild, a ploughman of national repute, who had won many major competitions, and his father was similarly mounted on one of the second pair of horses. Nosebags hung from the hames of all four horses, for they, too, had to take their midday feed out to the field where they were working. Both men said, 'Hullo', old Goodchild adding, 'Been earning your keep, then?' They didn't stop, as they wanted to get back to Biddles Farm, to water and unharness their horses. They then had to rub down and feed them, put down the straw bedding and top up the hayracks for the night before they could go and get their tea. Along with Charlie Coxhead from Lynch Hill, they had been ploughing The Long Acre, a narrow field of five to six acres that ran parallel to Biddles Lane. I had just been able to see the three teams at work from the far end of Forty Acres and a grand sight they made.

A good ploughman with a pair of horses could turn over an acre, sometimes fractionally more, in a day. I smiled smugly to myself as I sped along the lane towards Lynch Hill: three men and six horses hadn't ploughed as much ground in the day as I had with the tractor. I came up behind Charlie Coxhead, mounted like the Goodchilds, as he took his pair of Suffolk Punches back to the stable. They had only recently been acquired, replacing the pair of grey Shires

Charlie had previously worked. Edward Clifton-Brown, the estate owner, came from an old East Anglian family and favoured the breeds he had been used to since he was a child.

I called a cheery 'Good night' to Charlie as I sped past, causing his mount to shy and Charlie to swear as he grabbed the hames. As I reached the bottom of the hill, near the end of Lammas Wood, a couple of rats scuttled, squeaking across the road. Tawny owls called to each other, one quite close, the other away up the wood. I stopped to listen; I loved their distinctive cry. It is normally symbolised as 'to-whit-to-woo', but if one listens carefully it is more like 'hoo . . . hoo . . . hoooo'. A pleasing unobtrusive sound, once so much a part of our English countryside at night. There were, to my certain knowledge, two pairs that lived in and around the wood. As I stood listening, answering calls came from Bangles Spinney away to my right, and then another joined in from Lynch Hill Spinney, directly behind me. A moorhen called from the pond, only yards from where I stood, whilst several mallards flew overhead, quietly quacking, as they glided into Lammas pond. The evening was vibrant with sounds, so meaningful to those who know, often so scary to those who don't.

I climbed back onto my bike, and minutes later I was home, well pleased with myself, as I happily extolled the advantages of tractors over horses to father. He listened to my chattering, then smiled. 'You seem very full of yourself having done a day's work and, sadly, you're right. Tractors do get on with the work quicker than horses, but, unfortunately, such progress will decimate the countryside as we know it, alter our whole way of life and, worst of all, mean the loss of thousands of jobs from the land in the years to come.'

It was a theme I knew well: many of his friends said Father was an alarmist, others that he was an old backward-looking 'fuddy-duddy'. Certainly he was not the latter, for the Burnham

Grove Estate frequently featured in the farming press because of the modern methods employed. No, Father was a realist who had few, if any, illusions as to what the outcome of further mechanisation would mean, but like many of his generation, he knew he had to go along with it. However, I'm quite sure he did not visualise the extraordinary changes in both husbandry and technology that would revolutionise agriculture during his lifetime, totally change the look of the countryside and deplete the wildlife. He often said to me as a boy, 'Remember, we are only caretakers. The land is our heritage. Look after the land and it will look after you, never abuse it!'

The next morning, as I left home, snow was blowing in the wind. I tied an extra coat, a riding-mack, onto the carrier of my bike; it looked as though I might need it. By the time I reached Forty Acres, just before 7.00 a.m., Jack had already unsheeted the tractors and had them warming up. It seemed obvious that he was going to stick at it and get as much done as possible. Any hopes I had of knocking-off midday seemed problematical. It looked as though it was going to be an ideal afternoon for pigeon shooting too, but my instructions were clear, 'You do what Jack says'. The snow had stopped, but what little there had been lay white on the ground. Louring black clouds, away to the north, threatened more to come, and an icy wind gusted straight down the field. As I struggled into my mack, I was beginning to wonder if volunteering had been such a great idea, for the weather was far from inviting. By lunch I was frozen and envied the Goodchilds and Charlie Coxhead, whom I could see away in the distance, being able to walk behind their ploughs. At least they had some hope of keeping reasonably warm, even if their output wasn't as great as mine. Apart from the cold, the morning had not been improved by the fact that every time I headed up the field, into the wind, the exhaust fumes were blown back in my face.

It was a great relief to get on my bike and head back to Pound Cottage for my lunch – piping hot Irish stew, with loads of pearl barley, followed by chocolate steam pudding with clotted cream and sugar. Fortified, I returned to my labours, as on the previous day Jack was already at work. Thankfully he decided to knock-off at four o'clock and greatly relieved I headed for home. Monday I returned to my studies and Tom returned to his tractor. On reflection, one might get a greater output with a tractor, but horses were more fun, warmer and required a higher degree of skill – anyway, horses understood when one spoke to them, tractors just puffed out more exhaust fumes!

When I first took hold of a pair of plough lines (reins) and the handles of a plough, I could only have been about ten. The carter, who had been instructed to show me the rudiments of ploughing, walked the stubble beside me telling me what to do. At that time there was great competition between the horsemen as to whose charges looked the best and pride in having both horses and harness shining. Each man had his own corn bin, always locked. Every Friday evening the week's ration for all the stock was weighed out and recorded and then distributed to those concerned on Saturday mornings. A supply of rolled oats and bran was put up for every pair of horses. All received the same generous amount, but in spite of this Sam House's matching pair of brown Shires at Britwell always seemed to carry that bit more bloom than the others in the same stable. It didn't matter how hard they groomed their charges; the other carters could not get theirs to match Sam's.

Every Friday evening when the granary at Britwell was opened up, a number of men gathered, all keen to get the overtime. They worked under the watchful eye of Tom Bunce, better known to his workmates as 'Peg-leg' for he had a wooden leg, and made up the various rations. The granary went off at right angles to the big barn, the top floor being a loft, where grain, mostly oats, was carefully stored at a depth of some two to three feet and regularly turned by hand. The loft ran on over Sam House's kitchen, for he lived in the cottage that joined onto the end of the granary. On either side of the loft space was left to give easy access, both for turning and for checking that the grain was not overheating.

One Friday evening Tom Rose, who had called in to see that all was well, walked along to the end of the loft which adjoined Sam's home. Suddenly he saw a movement in the oats close to the end wall. At first he thought he was seeing things, but again the corn moved. It could be only a rat, or at least so Tom thought, although the granary was believed to be one hundred per cent ratproof. Gingerly, Tom dug down with his hands through some two feet of oats, and the next thing he knew was that the long blade of a carving knife slid up between his fingers, mercifully not cutting him. Once he'd got over the surprise, it did not take Tom long to put two and two together.

He left the granary, crossed the yard, crept down the side of Sam's cottage and peered through the kitchen window. There he saw Sam, standing on a chair, working a knife up and down through a crack in the wooden ceiling, as a steady trickle of oats made its way into a bucket he was holding in his other hand. The mystery as to why Sam's horses looked that much better than anyone else's was solved – they were getting extra oats.

Normally such a transgression, being looked upon as a somewhat ingenious and amusing ploy, would have led to only a mild reprimand, and that would have been the end of the matter. Sadly, however, when Tom knocked at the door and faced Sam with his misdeed, the latter flew into a rage, accused Tom of spying on him and, finally, took a swing at the foreman, who reported the incident to Father. Unfortunately Sam was not in the least contrite, became somewhat abusive to Father and said he was only helping himself to oats so that his horses looked the best. Reluctantly, Father sacked Sam, for although he was a good worker he couldn't condone his behaviour towards Tom.

There was, however, a happy ending. Sam immediately obtained a job as head horseman on a nearby farm, whose owner was very keen on Shires and had much admired Sam's when they won the best-turned-out pair at the previous South Bucks Ploughing Match. He contacted Father to see if he could buy them. As it was the start of the changeover to Suffolk Punches, a deal was quickly done, Sam was reunited with his beloved horses, two superb Suffolks, Sprey and Boxer, arrived at Britwell and, before a new horseman moved into the cottage, the kitchen ceiling was plastered!

# 5
# *The Ups and Downs of Harvest*

H ARVEST saw the culmination of the year's activities, the end product for the hours, indeed weeks, of work with teams of horses or with trusty, but oh-so-uncomfortable, tractors at ploughing and cultivating. It took three horses even on light land to pull a cultivator, or 'grubber' as it was locally known. Then there would be more hours harrowing and rolling, before, eventually, arriving at a seedbed. For winter corn, usually sown at the end of October or in November, the ground would be left rougher, theoretically to protect the seedlings from frost. Whether this really was the case I wouldn't like to say, but it meant that, in the spring, a further light harrowing and rolling was required. If the land was heavy clay (we had little of this on the estate), it was almost impossible to work up a winter seedbed during a wet season. In such cases, the field would be left for spring sowing, frost being adjudged the best 'tool' to break down heavy land into a nice friable condition. Back in the 1920s, 1930s and before, land was often referred to as being two-, three- or four-horse – that was the number of horses required to draw a single furrow plough. If it was four-horse it was really heavy, sticky clay, often good wheat land, but a devil to cultivate.

Artificial chemical manures were looked upon by most farmers as a supplement to dung, which after harvest was carted out from nearby clamps and spread by hand on the stubbles destined to be ploughed for winter wheat, or, in the spring, for root crops, such as potatoes, mangolds, swedes and kale. The three main chemical fertilisers, always known as 'artificials', were phosphate, potash and nitrogen, as indeed they still are. They were not available ready mixed to varying formulas, but came separately in the form of a coarse powder. These had to be mixed to the required proportions on a barn floor. Once the required number of bags had been emptied, the heap had to be turned at least three, if not four, times to make sure everything was blended correctly before being rebagged to take out to the fields. It was a backbreaking and boring job, which was never enhanced by the fact that, once mixed, the resulting 'brew' had to be applied in the shortest possible time, as any delay could bring about hydration and one was left with a gooey mess which could not be applied with a fertiliser spreader. However, most farmers were agreed that good, old-fashioned farmyard manure couldn't be bettered, although other organic material was used. For example a large number of houses were not on main drainage and the septic tanks had to be regularly emptied, the contents being a welcome addition to many a farmer's stubble before ploughing.

Another additive, and anyone within a radius of several miles would know when it had been used, was guano – the excrement of sea birds and shipped mostly from South America. It was a good fertiliser, but to say that it stank would be an understatement. I only remember it being used once on the estate. A generous dressing was given to a very poor field, Cants Hill, about half a mile from Edward Clifton-Brown's residence with devastating results. He and his wife departed, at very short notice, to their London house until the field was ploughed; whilst the secretary of the Burnham Golf Club, about the same distance in the opposite direction, seemed to live on the telephone complaining bitterly about the ghastly smell that pervaded the clubhouse. It was the first and last time that guano was used on the farms.

Preparing the land and actually seeding it was, by today's standards, a long and protracted operation as, too, was harvesting, but it got done, for there were plenty of workers and plenty of time to do it in. As one worker used to say, 'When God made time He made plenty of it.'

Having got the crop established, there could be many a problem between sowing and ricking. It was not unusual before the start of haymaking in the spring to have a gang of ten or a dozen men going through a field of corn, pulling wild oats. These were a menace if once truly established in a field, as they could ruin a sample of wheat for milling or, indeed, for seed. Thistles were another scourge, the seed often wind-borne for some considerable distance before coming to rest. When this happened a gang would be sent 'spudding'. A 'spud' was a flattened piece of iron, with a slightly curved neck, rather like a Dutch hoe, attached to a long handle, and one cut through the stem of the offending weed at ground level. 'Old Jay' would make up 'spuds' out of odd bits of iron.

These days, of course, both problems would be quickly dealt with by the application of a spray, which would undoubtedly achieve its objective, but, almost certainly, at the same time destroy a variety of insects and flora.

During the latter part of the 1930s, weeds were not the only thing causing damage to crops. The ancient and lovely forest of Burnham Beeches attracted more and more visitors. Londoners would catch a train to Burnham Beeches Station, not realising it was a good mile and a half to two mile walk from their objective. Their route was through the heart of the estate. Frequently, on a hot summer's day, they would decide to leave the road and set about having a picnic in the nearest field. The fact that it was standing corn, or a crop of hay, worried the majority not one iota. In fairness, in many cases, it was purely ignorance that led to their acts of vandalism, but not always. Such destruction was by no means limited to the Burnham Grove Estate. There was a much publicised case where a farmer near Hungerford in Berkshire came along one Sunday morning to find two cars had been driven out into the middle of a field of hay just about ready for mowing. Apart from the tracks of the cars, some thirty to forty square yards had been flattened and a picnic was in full swing. The farmer, not surprisingly, was irate and remonstrated with the offenders in the strongest possible terms. All he got was abuse and he was told by one of the men concerned (I'll call him 'Mr X) that all land was a gift from God and no one person had a right to claim it. The farmer, it seemed, showed great restraint, replying that that was an interesting theory and would 'Mr X' be so good as to put it in writing and, also, supply his name and address? This was readily agreed to by the bumptious 'Mr X', who it seemed lived in a very upmarket house in Richmond. The farmer thanked his unwanted visitor most courteously and departed.

The following Sunday 'Mr X' was awakened around 8.00 a.m. by the sound of much laughter coming from his garden. He looked out and there to his horror, he saw a wood fire burning merrily in the centre of his well-manicured lawn, over which he could see a woman frying breakfast, whilst three children played 'tig' through the herbaceous borders and a man sat, in a deck-chair, reading a paper. 'Mr X' let out a roar of indignation and demanded to know what the ****** hell was going on. The man quietly folded his paper, got up and walked towards the house. It was the farmer whom 'Mr X' had assured that 'all land was a gift from God and no one person had a right to claim it'. The police were called and, in due course, the matter went to court. It made headlines in the tabloid press, particularly after 'Mr X' had admitted his assertion regarding the ownership of land, something he could hardly refute in view of his signed declaration to this effect. The farmer and his family were found 'not guilty'. Truly a case of poetic justice!

None of the many rather similar incidents on the estate at Burnham ever ended up in court, but one, if it hadn't been for the intervention of Edward Clifton-Brown, most certainly would have. The harvest was nearly over, and just one piece of late-sown spring wheat in Forty Acres was left to cut. George Devonshire had been 'on watch' for poachers or other miscreants and was riding his bike along Deep Lane, heading for his bed, when he heard much hilarious laughter, music and saw light coming from the centre of the uncut wheat. He immediately went to investigate and found that two Bentleys and a Sunbeam had been driven out into the corn and parked, their lights being used to illuminate a midnight picnic. There were four young men, little more than boys, all in white tie and tails, and four girls in long evening dresses. As one of them said later, they were all slightly squiffy, resulting in them being very abusive to George, and one was even foolish enough to threaten him, not a wise thing to do, as he quickly learned.

Having taken their names and addresses and the cars' registration numbers, George shepherded them out onto Deep Lane and saw them back onto the public highway.

The following morning he reported the matter to Father, who was about to leave for Burnham Grove. In the course of conversation he told Clifton-Brown of the previous night's high jinks in Forty Acres and that the participants had been warned by Devonshire that they would undoubtedly be taken to court. On hearing the names of the offenders, E. C. B. vetoed this, saying that two of the young men were the sons of good friends of his in the City and that he would deal with the matter. In due course an apology and a cheque, that more than compensated for the damage, arrived at the estate office, together with two £5 notes for George. The latter was delighted, for it was equal to about five weeks' wages and he assured Father, that as far as he was concerned, they could come back anytime!

In addition to vandals and weeds, rabbits and wood pigeons were a menace. They would attack all corn crops, together with a number of root ones. The constant war that was waged against them brought in a certain amount of income, but it in no way paid for the damage they did. The price of rabbits varied from ls to ls 6d and the going rate for pigeons was 6d. When cooked up with vegetables, these produced a cheap and appetising meal for a few pence per head.

I always enjoyed harvest time. There was so much activity, such a sense of urgency, and every rick completed was a significant achievement, although I doubt old 'Gunner' Stingmore looked at it that way. More often than not, as he stepped off the ladder coming down from topping a rick (as builder he would be the last man down), he'd spit on the ground and announce to no one in particular, 'Thar's another b****r finished.' Harvest was not only about gathering in the grain; it was also the time when a major offensive was launched against the rabbit population which inhabited the fields of corn. From an early age, first standing with Bob Hedges and then later taking a corner on my own, I would be one of the guns shooting the hordes of rabbits that fled from what had been their feeding ground. Hordes was not an exaggeration. The most I ever remember from one field of wheat was something just over four hundred. However, I must admit that was exceptional, which was just as well, for the damage they had done was horrendous.

Of the many occasions I shot rabbits from the corn, one particular evening remains vividly in my memory. It was around 6.30 p.m. and the binders were coming to the end of a field of spring-sown wheat, close to Lynch Hill Farmyard. It had been a difficult time with endless thunderstorms. The end of the cutting was in sight, when, yet again, heavy black clouds started to build up to the west, and what was more, they were heading our way – it seemed a certainty that we were in for yet another storm. It was the last field to cut and half to three-quarters of an hour would mean the binders could be cleaned, serviced and put away for another year. Charlie Coxhead, on seeing the approaching storm, wisely pulled out, unhitched his horses and, having covered the binder with a tarpaulin, headed for the stables, leaving Jack Keen, with a tractor-drawn binder, to finish what was left. Bob Hedges, George Devonshire, Bill Yeoman (the head gamekeeper) and I were strategically placed with our guns at each corner. Our job was just as important as that of any of the men busily stocking the sheaves as they were chucked out by the binder, for, as I have said, the control of rabbits was paramount. Throughout the country they did millions of pounds worth of damage annually and, in those days, a million was a lot of money. The corn being cut was full of rabbits and when the gang had stopped for tea, before we had ours, we, the guns, gathered up over a hundred that we'd shot.

The rumbling of the storm grew ever nearer and it was obvious, to one and all, that Bill Yeoman was far from happy. He was heartily disliked by the rest of the staff; it was generally accepted that he was 'gutless' and George Devonshire had openly told him that a small boy, trespassing in search of birds' nests, could put him to flight, let alone a poacher. He was, also, well known for his dislike of getting wet, but he needn't have worried. The thunder grew ever closer and the sky was almost continually streaked with lightning. Once more up and down the remaining corn was all that was needed to see the end of the cutting, and at this point the storm arrived right overhead – there wasn't a spot of rain, but the atmosphere seemed charged with electricity. The lightning was as awesome as the crashes of thunder were frightening. I was following the binder, down to where Bill Yeoman stood, as it cut the last swath. Suddenly there was a blinding flash, followed by a terrifying crack as a wych elm, some hundred and fifty yards away, was split in two, as easily as Tom Hanks would have split a length of willow with a 'molly', leaving the two halves burning like spent Roman candles. To say that it was scary would be a major understatement! I kept repeating to myself what I had always been told, namely, that one was safer out in the middle of a field than under a tree, but, I must admit, I found it hard to convince myself.

We were nearly at the end when there was a near-deafening clap of thunder, which seemed to be directly over my head, and lightning sizzled past my ear, or so it seemed. About a hundred thousandth of a second later Yeoman's gun flew from his hands. Poor Bill, he was unhurt, but as Jack Adaway said, he screamed 'like an ole pig havin' its throat cut' as he fled towards the binder Charlie Coxhead had sheeted up and dived in under the tarpaulin. Cutting was finished, as was stocking, before Bill Yeoman peeped out, but he would come no further, although, in turn, we all told him the storm had passed and it was safe. George retrieved Bill's gun, miraculously unharmed. Even this good news would not persuade Bill to leave his hidey-hole, and it was only when we had gathered up all the rabbits that he emerged.

On looking back I suppose it was not surprising that we never saw Yeoman in the harvest field again if there was the slightest likelihood of there being a thunder storm and, really, who could blame him!

Heavy rainstorms before harvest were the bane of every arable farmer's life, for, as straw was much longer than it is today, whole fields could be flattened in a matter of hours. When this happened it truly became hell's own job to cut, or, indeed, to even salvage part of the crop. With modern machinery, flattened corn is, normally, no major problem, but in the 1930s and earlier, it was a terrible worry, often leading to serious financial difficulties for farmers. More than one went bust, in the depression of the 1930s, because of atrocious weather at harvest time. Sometimes, however, for those of us keen on shooting, this was a plus, because laid corn became ideal feeding ground for the vast flocks of wood pigeons which inhabited the countryside.

I remember one summer I was disc harrowing a section of Big Field, which was being fallowed, next to some twenty acres of black winter oats which adjoined The Belt. Four days earlier it had been a magnificent sight and had been awarded first prize in a competition for the best field of winter oats in the south of the county. The night after it had been assessed by the judges we had a horrendous storm, and next morning virtually the entire acreage was flattened. As the old Fordson toiled up and down the field I could see pigeons, hundreds and hundreds of them, descending on the battered crop. That evening, when I got home, I told Father. Much to my delight he said that next day I was to take my decoys, gun and a good supply of cartridges and see if I could not only reduce the number of marauders, but, also, by so doing, persuade them to seek new feeding grounds.

I was making my way along The Belt soon after 8.00 a.m., the grey sky already blue with pigeons. I was well loaded down with some two hundred and fifty cartridges, decoys and, most important, 'Woodie'. The latter was my secret weapon. She was a wood pigeon who had fallen out of a nest in Bangle's Spinney as a fledgeling and, when I found her, was apparently unharmed. I had taken her home and put her in the nest-box with a couple of my Racing Homer chicks of around the same size. Much to my surprise, the parent birds accepted her and reared her. She was no trouble to tame and would let me pick her up without struggling and would happily sit on my wrist and eat corn from the palm of my hand. However, rearing 'Woodie' was not entirely for altruistic reasons; there was a purpose. An extremely knowledgeable pigeon shooter, who lived only a few miles away, taught me how to work a live decoy. My friend helped me to make and fit a harness to Woodie'. This went around her breast, joining up on her back between the wings. Having done this, on my friend's advice, I asked 'Old Jay' to make me up a 'launcher' from the lightest iron rod he had. This was about four feet six inches high, with a short arm set at right angles at the top, with an eye in the end. Through this one threaded a fine line, attached it to the harness and could then hoist up one's decoy bird. I gave 'Woodie' a few training sessions on the lawn at home and in no time at all she would allow herself to be hauled up and, when the line was slackened fly out in a most convincing and natural way, thus providing a lure that few, if any, passing pigeons could resist, as seeing the live pigeon fly out on the feed-ground, they seemed to lose their normal wariness and would swoop in

Having made a hide, put out my decoys and organised 'Woodie', who incidentally had become immune to the sound of gunfire,

I was quickly in business. Pigeons came in what seemed like a never-ending stream to guzzle on the oats. The wooden decoys were a sufficient attraction leaving 'Woodie' free to feed or take a nap. I shot until the barrels of my gun were too hot to hold. Then things suddenly went quiet, almost as though the 'enemy' had retired to regroup. I left my hide to collect the pigeons I had shot, not bothering to count them, for, by the time I was picking up the last of the bag, a fresh attack was starting. It was well into the afternoon before 'Woodie' was called upon to earn her keep. By this time the marauders were becoming distinctly wary; even so the majority succumbed to the allure of 'Woodie'. It reminded me of the mythological stories of sailors being lured to their doom by the singing of the sirens. At last I ran out of cartridges so, having given 'Woodie' a drink and put her in her box I started to collect the rest of my bag – one hundred and eighty-three, far more than I could possibly carry, but still only a very small percentage of those that had flown in to gorge themselves to near-bursting point. Pigeons are voracious feeders and the damage that wood pigeons did to farm crops was, in those days, second only to rabbits.

It was a blisteringly hot day, as it had been since the day after the storm that had flattened the oats, so I decided to take 'Woodie' and the rest of my stuff home. I then returned to Lynch Hill Farm, got out the old car used for hay sweeping and drove up to The Belt – there wasn't a pigeon in sight. It seemed I had provided the deterrent that had been needed. My 'bag', which were all lovely plump birds, was purchased by Macfisheries in Maidenhead at sixpence each, to be quickly sold with a fifty per cent mark-up.

Seeing off the pigeons was not my last encounter with the oats. There was no way that they could be cut with a binder, for they were so flattened and tangled as to make this impossible. Father and Tom Rose debated the matter and decided that the only hope of salvaging anything was to try to cut the tangled crops with mowing machines. It took two days of hot dusty work to achieve this and then only with a gang of us lifting the straw with forks so the mower blades could get under it. The weather held good and it was decided to set up the threshing tackle in the field and deal with what could be salvaged there and then. This was an almost unprecedented happening, for there was an old saying, strongly adhered to in those days, that oats, when cut, should hear the church bells ring three times before being ricked, otherwise they'd overheat. I spent a day and a half sweeping what was left of what should have been a super crop to the thresher. The heat and dust was almost indescribable and by the time we'd finished, we were all nearly as black as the oats! Our efforts yielded just over fourteen hundredweights to the acre – less than half what it would have been had the crop remained standing.

A few days later I was passing that way and saw that the pigeons were back in force. When the tangled oats were mown, many heads of grain were cut off, and these were too small to pick up with the sweep. I took a walk out across the stubble and realised that there must still be several hundredweights of grain left to the acre. I had recently read an article in the *Farmer and Stockbreeder* about growing catch crops. I knew that that section of Big Field was destined for spring barley. So, why not cut it up well with disc harrows, which would not only produce a tilth, but would spread the oats around. If we added some turnip seed, the crop should produce some additional feed for the Hampshire Down flock. It certainly made sense to me and I put my idea to Father. He was quite enthusiastic.

'Good idea. You can take the spare tractor and start discing this afternoon.'

That hadn't been my intention: I had envisaged Jack Keen or Tom Brookling doing it, or possibly one of the farm pupils. I

*Suffolk mares on maternity leave.*

*Gathering the harvest the old-fashioned way.*

*Shaping a chair seat with an adze.*

*Tailing lambs and then preparing the tails for cooking.*

*Ready to start milking in Lynch Hill cow barn – at the time one of the most advanced in the country.*

BACK ROW, LEFT TO RIGHT: *Gregory Meek and Jim Light (head herdsman); George Claridge and Ken Light.*

*The fruits of our labour: prizes won at Burnham Flower Show and in the 'Fancy' section.*

*The Supreme Champion pen of sheep at the 1936 Smithfield Fatstock Show (Southdown and Hampshire Down crosses), shown by the author and two others (see page 112).*

Tom Rose, foreman (far left), with some of the estate staff in the 1930s.

Goliath, the Dexter steer that was stopped from being exhibited at Smithfield because of foot and mouth disease on a nearby farm.

The author, aged 13, with Bridget, about to set off on a day's trout fishing on the Torridge.

Fred Goodchild with some of the Tamworth sows at Biddles Farm.

Burnham Prim Lad being gingerly approached by Leslie Wood's daughter Patricia; Cecil Twist and the author are to the right. Note the hayrick in the background.

*Building a rick.*

*Thatching.*

*George Devonshire and Bob Hedges building a butt for partridge shooting, Big Field, 1934.*

*Pound Cottage, the author's home. Two old cottages knocked into one and added to.*

*The author aged 18 about to go for a ride in Burnham Beeches.*

Harry Wadman and Harry Jaycock about to load ram lambs going
off to the sales.

Part of the famous Burnham flock of Hampshire Downs, being folded
over Montgomery red clover and Italian rye grass. Note hurdles
made on the estate.

*Lynch Hill Farm and the farmhouse where Jack Keen lived.
In the background are a pair of cottages occupied by
Bob Hedges and Charlie Coxhead.*

*Jack Keen mowing a heavy one-year ley, which would have
been undersown with spring barley.*

*War or no war, pedigree livestock breeding goes on. The winning pen of eight ram lambs from the Burnham flock at the Salisbury Ram Fair in 1940. The staff are augmented by members of the Women's Land Army, which did such a superb job throughout the war.*

had intended, when I'd had lunch, to take 'Woodie' and the rest of my gear and thin out the pigeons yet again. Me and my big mouth! However, orders were orders and Father did not expect, or encourage, arguments once he'd made a decision. The sun was still blazing as the old Fordson, the only one left on spadelug wheels, chugged up and down the field, making heavy going of its task, for I had the discs set to achieve the maximum cut. By the following evening I had the best tilth possible. A quick run over with a ring-roller and it would be ready for sowing. On hearing this Father had said, 'Fine. I've arranged with Tom Rose to have Ted Wilmott there with two seed-barrows tomorrow morning.' Ted was an expert in the use of these, but why two? I quickly got my answer.

'It was your idea, so I feel it only right you should see the job through to the end. Anyway, you've never used a seed-barrow, so I thought it a good time for you to learn.' The actual seed box was, if I remember correctly, eighteen feet. There was a central spindle, fitted with little brushes; this was geared to the main wheel and the seed was pushed out through holes that could be adjusted to sow the required quantity of seed, in this case six pounds to the acre. After explaining about moving one's marker upon reaching the headland so as to ensure keeping straight, Ted said he'd do one round with me and then he'd make a start on the opposite side. It was hard sweaty work pushing the barrow, for the ground, even after rolling, was rough, but it wasn't quite as dull and tedious as I had anticipated. As I took a breather by The Belt, a sparrowhawk came winging down over the trees scattering the small birds that inhabited it in wild confusion. A cock chaffinch, stupidly, broke cover only feet from where I stood. The hawk dived, proving more than able to match every twist and turn of its fleeing victim, which it grasped whilst in full flight and carried over the trees. As I made my way back across the field, a brood of partridges landed between Ted and me. Every turn of the field produced something new to watch and, as a result, my sowing was not as straight as it might have been.

We'd been plodding up and down for about two hours when, as I approached The Belt, a hare came racing out, running straight towards me. On seeing me, 'puss' momentarily stopped, but only momentarily, for a lurcher burst out of the cover in hot pursuit. Its quarry turned back from whence it'd come; the lurcher was equally quick, seeming to 'turn on a sixpence' and continued its course. I sprinted to The Belt and pushed my way through to the other side, just in time to see the lurcher grab the hare. One agonised scream and it was all over, the hare hanging limply from its pursuer's jaws. A hundred yards or so away, out on the stubble, was a man. I recognised him at once, Jim Sloane, an inveterate poacher. He was a menace. I don't think he did it purely for the money, like many; he was addicted – poaching was like a drug to him, he just couldn't stop. Rose, his lurcher bitch, was nearly back to him when he spotted me heading towards him. He grabbed the hare and started to run towards Deep Lane, with me in hot pursuit. He reached the lane about forty yards ahead of me and turned towards Biddles Farm, only to run straight into the arms of George Devonshire, who took over from there on, whilst I made my way back to my seed-barrow.

The following morning I rolled the oat ground with a flat roll behind the old car and the job was done. The harvest was over and all the corn safely ricked. Three nights later the weather broke and we had a spell of warm showery weather, ideal for germinating both the oats and the turnips which, in due course, produced some excellent feed for the sheep.

Two weeks' later I had to appear at Burnham Magistrates Court to give evidence against Jim Sloane. It didn't take long, for, with a shrug of his shoulders, he pleaded guilty as charged. Old Mr Inkpen, chairman of the bench, usually most lenient, must have got out of bed the wrong side that morning. To everyone's surprise, he fined Jim £12 and gave him two weeks in which to pay; otherwise he'd be sent to jail to do six weeks hard labour and that, in those days, was no picnic. It was something of a coincidence that, starting that night, there was an outbreak of chicken stealing in the district. This went on for about ten days and stopped the day Jim paid his fine!

# 6

## *Blaze*

HORSES, both work and riding, played no small part in my life back in the 1930s. Although I did not own either a pony or a horse, I was well compensated by having access to Billy Oliver's riding school-cum-livery stable at East Burnham, which quite literally joined the north-eastern corner of the estate. Billy came to see Father, I suppose it must have been in the late '20s, to seek permission to ride along the estate's private roads and, when possible, gallop horses in some of the fields. With the full agreement of Edward Clifton-Brown, Father gave consent, but with one proviso, namely that my brother, Ralph, and I could ride, whenever possible, for free. 'Free' was certainly a misnomer for, by the time I was into my teens, I'd sweated blood grooming horses, cleaning tack and learning every aspect of stable management, which in the years to come stood me in good stead. I was lucky, for Billy's father took a liking to me. He was an ex-steeplechase jockey, as tough as they come, and he decided to 'school' me himself. His methods, too, were tough, for he was not adverse to giving me a quick 'tickle up', as he put it, with his riding whip if I wasn't paying attention or was doing something wrong. The result was that I learned fast and, by the mid-1930s, was entrusted to ride out on most of the horses at livery.

It was around this time that E. C. B., when visiting relations who had an estate in East Anglia, bought a four-year-old Suffolk Punch, by the name of Blaze, off a neighbour of his kinsman. Blaze was well named: he was a lovely deep chestnut with a long white blaze running right down his face. He was indeed a fine looking boy, nearly seventeen hands high. He was supposedly fully broken and quiet in all gears.

When he arrived at Burnham he was superfluous to requirements and, as there wasn't a vacant stall in the Britwell stables, he went to Lynch Hill. By then, which was the spring after my first serious ploughing venture, pneumatic tyred wheels had been fitted to one of the two Fordson tractors, giving greater mobility, and a third tractor purchased, resulting in a pair of horses being sold. This meant that Charlie Coxhead the horseman had the Lynch Hill stables to himself. Tom Rose reported that Charlie wasn't too pleased at having an extra horse to care for. Further he, Tom, thought Charlie was scared stiff of his new charge. Apparently when Charlie had taken him out to water, Blaze had squealed, reared and kicked his hind legs high in the air, since when Charlie had been carting water to him in a bucket, refusing to take him out of the stable. When I heard this I thought, 'Ah, this sounds like a bit of fun.' I'd recently 'backed' a three-year-old at Billy's stable and, quietly, thought myself no end of a fine fellow when it came to horses. Indeed, I had greatly enjoyed helping to break two Suffolks that had been bred on the estate and had learned a lot from this experience. I immediately volunteered to take Blaze out, lunge him and then set him to work pulling a flat roller. Father, after a moment's hesitation, agreed, providing Tom Rose was there to help me get started.

The following afternoon, as soon as I'd finished lunch, I headed off to Lynch Hill, with a goodly supply of sugar in my pocket. I entered the stall, quietly talking, leant against the manger and began patting Blaze and rubbing him behind his ears; then I tried him with a lump of sugar – a great success. I spent ten minutes to a quarter of an hour 'making friends', at the end of which time I felt pretty certain there was no real vice in him. Although there was no sign of Tom, I decided to start getting Blaze harnessed. After carefully closing the stable door, I fetched a collar which I thought would fit from the harness room, slipped it over his head and twisted it into position. He snorted a bit, but stood quietly in the stall. So far so good. Then I put a bridle on him and eased the bit into his mouth. The bridle, like all cart-horse ones, had blinkers, so he could no longer see behind him. I then fetched the pad (saddle), breeching, etcetera and plumped it on his back. I felt, rather than saw, Blaze tense himself, but he never moved. I reached under him, caught the girth and gently cinched it up, but not too tightly. Warning lights were flashing: something about Master Blaze wasn't quite kosher, although he'd done nothing to really cause my mistrust. Carefully I tied a ploughline to the noseband of the bridle to use as a lunging rein, talking quietly all the time, for I could see from his eyes that Blaze wasn't happy. At last I was ready, but there was still no sign of Tom. However, with the crass impetuousness of youth, I was sure I could manage without him and, so, tried to back Blaze out of the stall.

That was when the fireworks started. Anyone who hasn't been in the comparatively confined space of a cart-horse's stall with about a ton of horseflesh trying to do gymnastics will have a job to relate to the situation in which I found myself – it is, I can assure readers, a very stimulating experience – it stimulates one's reflexes to an almost unbelievable degree to duck and weave to avoid flying iron-clad hooves and being crushed against the side of the stall. One really hasn't time to be scared, as all one's attention is centred on survival. After a minute or two (it seemed like eternity) Blaze ceased hurling himself around and, eyes staring, nostrils flared and shaking like a jelly, he stood as though rooted to the spot, half out of the stall. Still holding the lunge rein I slithered gently round the end of the partition and into the passage, giving a sigh of relief as I did so, for now I could get out of the gelding's way if he decided to have another go. Quietly I paid out the rein until I reached the stable door, which I opened. Talking softly all the time, I slowly returned towards Blaze and began to ease his head round into the passage. Hesitantly he took a step, then another, and we reached the door. I had just slipped through and round to the side as he burst out behind me, when wham – the show was on again. He stood straight up on his hind legs, flailing the air before crashing down and kicking both hind feet high above his head. Fortunately I had done the girth up sufficiently tight so that the pad did not slip. I prayed the rolling hitch, with which I had attached the plough line to the centre of the noseband, wouldn't slip. As long as that held, I could pull Blaze's head round, and I was, supposedly, in control. If he got his head out straight he was gone.

At that moment Tom arrived. He was, to say the least, explicit in his comments on my having gone ahead without him, but, having delivered a broadside, he hooked the short rein back over the hames and then between us we led the cavorting, snorting Blaze across the lane into the rickyard, where we lunged him for about twenty minutes. We then pushed him back, attached the reins to the bit and drove him forward; there seemed to be no problems either way. Tom grinned, 'You'll be all right now. Reckon he was just a bit stable fresh. He hasn't done any work for four or five days. I'll help you get him hooked up to the roller, then I must be off.' The roller was a medium weight flat-roll and had a seat fixed out behind it, with an iron rest for one's feet. I backed Blaze up to the roller, Tom lowered the shafts and we made everything fast. I gathered the reins and climbed up onto the seat, Tom led Blaze forward and out onto the lane, and it seemed as though butter wouldn't melt in his mouth. Tom made his adieus, warning me, as we left, never to try anything like I had on my own again, not unless I wanted to meet a sudden and premature death.

As he walked away I flapped the reins on Blaze's back and called out, 'Come on boy, gid-up.' Nothing happened. I shook the reins several more times, but there was no response. Then, suddenly, for no apparent reason, Blaze came to life and I got a greater response than I'd been looking for. As soon as the roller started to crunch and rattle on the gravel surface of the lane, he set his jaw and broke into a brisk trot, then into a canter, the roller bouncing off the road like hailstones. Hanging on for dear life, my legs braced against the footrest, I heaved on the reins, calling 'Whoa, Whoa,' but it was to no avail. I began to panic, for in another two to three hundred yards we would be arriving at a T junction. The canter had become nearly a gallop and there was no way we could negotiate a right-angled turn at the speed we were travelling. Seconds later, much to my relief, I saw that the gate leading into a section of Big Field was open and beyond it was some fifteen acres of fallow. Whilst Blaze's brakes seemed to be nonexistent, he did seem to have some steerage left, but it was going to be close, for the gateway was nine feet wide, the roller eight. If we caught one of the posts, solid oak, set about four feet into the ground, I was going to be catapulted out into the field at the best, or flattened by a half-ton roller at the worst. With about two inches to spare, we passed through the opening at a brisk canter, which quickly slowed to a trot and then a walk as we surged out into the field, which had been given a good, deep grubbing with a cultivator just a couple of days before. I pulled on the reins and cried, 'Whoa boy, whoa.' Sides heaving, the gelding did as he was bid. I jumped down and went to his head and started to fuss him; after a minute or so he began to nuzzle my pocket – I still had some sugar left and this he seemed to know.

Tom Rose arrived, puffing and blowing. He'd run up the lane behind me. 'Are you all right? I thought you'd be killed. Mad b****y horse, he ought to be shot before he really does for someone.'

'I'm fine, so is Blaze. Personally I don't think there's any vice in him, but I'd have a sizeable bet that he showed a bit of spirit when they, whoever they may be, started to break him as a two-year-old and got scared and left him.'

That evening Father phoned the man from whom E. C. B. had bought Blaze, who, after much prevaricating admitted that what I had thought was right. They'd started to break the colt, as he was then, but he was too much for them and, after he had broken someone's leg they had turned Blaze out in the field and, except for gelding him the following summer, hadn't touched him waiting for a suitable soft touch to come along to sell him to. This had turned out to be Edward Clifton-Brown. Under normal circumstances Father would have sent the gelding back and demanded the return of the purchase price, £80, which was, in any case, away over the true market value. However, it is always unwise to make the boss look a fool and to tell him he had been thoroughly duped would have been the height of folly. After much haggling, talk of the vendor obtaining money under false pretences and threats of solicitors, the previous owner of Blaze reluctantly agreed to refund £40.

For the next few weeks, any spare time I had, when I wasn't studying, was spent furthering Blaze's education. He and I quickly developed a rapport and for several days he rolled the fallow having, I might add, learned to proceed there at a more acceptable speed. Then it was time for some serious and productive work. Tom and Father decided that wireworm were playing the very devil with the barley in Nobb's Crook ('cuckoo barley' the old hands called it, as it was sown in April) and that a light rolling would be the appropriate treatment. Blaze and I got the job. The roller I was to take was lighter than the one used on the fallow and it had no seat, so it was a case of walking and driving and, as the field was about thirty-eight acres, that was going to be quite a lot of walking. Father told me I was to watch out for green plover scrapes (nests) as E. C. B. wanted a few dozen eggs and I was to collect any that I could. Plover eggs were considered quite a delicacy and the 'boss' liked to take them up to London to present to some of his City friends. There were, of course, countless thousands of green plover throughout the country at that time, their numbers not yet drastically depleted by endless spraying of the land with insecticides and the use of current-day farm machinery that has little or no respect for nature or the environment.

Green plovers are delightful, lovely birds, and the males' territorial display in the spring is truly spectacular. They rise slowly, then climb steadily before executing a wonderfully controlled spiralling dive, which culminates in a sudden upward twist and great fluttering of wings, so fast that it produces a sort of buzzing sound – almost like an agitated bee! If one approaches their nest, which is no more than a scrape in the ground, lined with a little grass and, incidentally, made by the cock bird they will mob the intruder with great intensity. If one hasn't already spotted the nest, this is a great giveaway. When we, that is I or the gamekeepers, collected eggs we never touched a nest with four, which is a normal clutch, for the chances were they had already started to incubate. We always left one in the nest if there were two or three and then, normally, the hen bird would continue and lay a full clutch.

The first afternoon I moved into Nobb's Crook to start rolling, the sun was shining, larks were hovering high overhead, warbling happily, before slowly sinking back to earth, whilst plovers swooped and dived over the length and breadth of the field. I decided to lead Blaze, rather than drive him, so that I could watch out for nests. Leading by now had reached a stage where it simply meant walking by his head. As I moved into position he nuzzled the right-hand pocket of my jacket, the one I kept the sugar in. Laughing, I patted him, told him he learned quickly and gave him the last two lumps I had left. We strode up and down the field, but there was nothing monotonous about it, for in the country there is always something of interest to watch. At one stage I spotted two common shrews having a real 'ding-dong'; they were so intent on their battle that they paid no attention to me, or indeed to Blaze and the roller. It seemed that they were combining every martial art ever known to man, as they jumped, circled, kicked, became locked together, biting before breaking away and circling like a couple of boxers I had been watching for several minutes before I spotted what I presumed was the reason for the skirmish, a third shrew crouched nearby, one had to surmise a female over whom the 'boys' were doing battle for her favours. Neither seemed to be winning, so I moved on, halting every so often to circumnavigate a nest, which, according to the number of eggs, either remained untouched or added one or two to the ever-growing collection in my left pocket. By late afternoon the latter could take no more and I started putting eggs in my right-hand one.

At just after 4.30 p.m. I took Blaze out from between the shafts to head back to Lynch Hill. As I turned to close the field gate Blaze must have had his mind on sugar, for I suddenly felt a hefty bump from his nose against my 'sugar' pocket. At the same time there was a sickening squelch as half a dozen or more, plover's eggs became scrambled. Cursing volubly, I pulled out a handful of dripping egg and held it towards Blaze. 'Now look what you've done, you stupid ninny.' Blaze pricked his ears, blew down his nostrils, it was almost a whinny. As he stretched his neck out, his soft velvety lips covered my hand as he sucked up the egg. He obviously liked it, for he even tried to eat the lining of my pocket as I turned it inside out to remove as much of the 'omelette' as I could.

A few months later poor old Tom, the oldest horse on the estate and stabled at Britwell, came to the end of his working days. Blaze moved to the main stable and became a fully integrated member of the work force, but he always remained my friend. In the summer, when he was out at grass, I only had to call and he'd come galloping up the field to me, rear up, his great iron-clad feet clanging together before he dropped down and immediately investigated my right pocket. Cupboard love? Possibly, but I like to think not entirely.

# 7

# A Touch of Dentistry

IT was not long after I started studying with the Rev
Barrington-Baker that Father decided I would profit from
some afternoons and free days spent at Biddles Farm, where
herds of Berkshire and Tamworth pigs were maintained. I wasn't
too keen, cattle and horses being my main interests, but orders
were orders. The Berkshires were by far the larger herd, much in
demand as porkers, and to look at they were most attractive, being
black with pricked ears, a white blaze down the face, white feet
with short white socks and a white tip to their well-curled tails.

The piglets, at two to three weeks, were delightful little things and, like any baby pig, given the opportunity made wonderful pets.

Biddles farmyard, with the exception of the stables and cart shed, was given over entirely to pigs. A large yard, originally built for cattle, accommodated some 25 to 30 in-pig sows and gilts, and the loose boxes were converted into farrowing units, or used for housing the stock boars. Maiden gilts and those recently served lived in half-acre grass runs, with large wooden pig arks to sleep in. Young boars, being run on for sale, were similarly housed. The runs covered the major portion of Gorse Field. In addition, in the farmyard, the old tithe barn was divided into good-sized pens for the Tamworth/Berkshire cross store pigs, very popular for both pork and bacon. It is sad that both these breeds, much sought after in the 1920s and 1930s, are now designated as rare breeds. In addition to the buildings already mentioned there was a specially constructed farrowing house.

All this was far removed from a modern-day piggery with sows in farrowing crates, etcetera. Even the stock boars had exercise paddocks, which they were walked out to, on fine days, by Fred Goodchild, the head pigman. Most of the boars were exhibited at agricultural shows and so were quite used to being driven. Fred was exceptional at his job. He had a unique understanding and affinity with his charges, and he was a great enthusiast when it came to showing and very proud of the herds for which he was responsible. He was one of six Goodchilds who worked on the estate, father and five sons. Fred was assisted by his youngest brother, Albert, who, whilst a good pigman, hadn't that certain something that makes an outstanding stockman like Fred.

The first afternoon that I 'reported for duty', I was warmly welcomed by Fred. 'Glad you've come, we've a nice little job for the next hour or so. Reckon the stores and porkers, in the barn, have worms. Goodness knows where they got them from, but they have, so they'll all have to be drenched.' The normal one with which pigs become infected is a species of roundworm, *Ascaris suilla*, about five to seven inches in length and a creamy white in colour – not very beautiful! This sounded as though it might be fun. I had anticipated something boring, like mucking out sties: when you've mucked out for one animal you've no more to learn, as the only thing that changes is the smell and with pigs that's not for the better!

Albert and I were to do the catching and holding, as well as marking each one when Fred had dosed it. Marking is important, as one doesn't want to treat the same pig twice. This was done with a raddle stick, a sort of solidified paint. When a pig had been treated, a stripe a few inches long would be made on its back. The medicine was a preparation called Santonin, which Fred mixed with water. The first two or three pens were little more than weaners, which, once caught, we could hold in our arms. Before we started Fred offered me a rubber apron, which reached from high on my chest to down below my knees. Albert donned a similar one. I was quickly to learn that thoroughly upset pigs are not too fussy what they do when caught, and one has to clasp them, metaphorically, to the bosom, as they utter piercing squeals into one's ear. Fred's offer of the apron was quickly understood.

The last pen contained porkers of 100 to 110 lbs weight – a really lively bunch. Like the previous lots these had to be held up in a corner with a hurdle and roped – not a noose around their necks, but a rope, with a slip knot, in their mouths around the top jaw and pulled up tight, so one could, with a little bit of luck, both hold them and open their mouths. The noise was continuous, strident and jarring to the nerves – they just didn't want to take their medicine. I was interested in the way Fred administered this to the bigger pigs. He had a boy's old leather boot with most of the toe area cut away, and he stuffed this into the protesting pig's mouth and poured away – most effective. When we'd finished, I glanced down at my apron: I was very glad I'd had it on!

Something which had intrigued me whilst we'd been so busy dealing with the pigs was the steady stream of swallows in and out of the barn to their nests, feeding their young. Neither our presence, nor the ghastly noise, seemed in any way to disturb them. Swallows, house martins and swifts were numerous around all the farm buildings on the estate, at least the first two were. I can only remember swifts at Lynch Hill, where they arrived annually from Africa, ten days or a fortnight later than the swallows and martins. Swifts are not exactly prolific breeders for, normally, they only have one brood, usually limited to two, or three at the most, whereas the swallows will lay certainly two, frequently three, clutches of eggs of four to six each time. It always struck me that the swifts came an awful long way just to lay a couple of eggs, but one has to assume that Mother Nature knows what she is doing. They are intriguing little birds, for they never seem to land on the ground, doing virtually everything on the wing, including mating, and if they do land, they have considerable difficulty in becoming airborne again. They drink whilst flying and it fascinated me the way they would come in low over the big horse trough and take a drink as they skimmed over the surface. Once I found one near the trough flapping about on the ground. Whether it had misjudged its swoop over the water and hit the edge, thus finishing up on the ground, I'll never know. Anyway I was too quick for it and, as it struggled frantically to get airborne, caught it. I stroked it gently, for which act of friendship it grabbed one of my fingers with its needlelike toenails. It was like pricking one's finger with about half a dozen pins! I had read how strong these toenails were, enabling them to cling to the walls of buildings where their nest holes were – now I had proof positive. I tossed it gently up into the air and, to my relief, it flew off.

After we'd finished the worming Fred asked me the time. I pulled out my Ingersol Crown pocket watch (very reliable and costing 5s). 'Exactly half-three.'

'Good. We can start feeding.'

The meal for the pigs was mixed with water to a consistency which made it easy to pour and equally easy for the pigs to slurp down at a great rate: they seemed to suck up food rather like a high-powered vacuum cleaner. I was 'armed' with a galvanised swing water barrel on rubber-tyred wheels. I suppose it held 25 to 30 gallons, into which I was told to put so many buckets of the mix, and after receiving precise instructions as to how much to ladle out, I started feeding the sows with litters. By the time we'd finished and I left for home, my head was positively splitting, first from all the yells of fright from the pigs as they were caught and dosed and then the squeals of anticipation from the matrons awaiting their tea.

Over the weeks that followed, working with the pigs became fairly humdrum, but I was learning all the time and that was the object of the exercise. I was also making a few bob on the side, for where there were pigs there were rats, and Biddles was no exception. Rats' tails, handed in at the estate office, were worth tuppence each and had for some years been a source by which I managed to supplement my pocket-money. The old cattle yard, used for in-pig sows, was a great hunting ground once feeding was over. The first evening that I tried my luck with my 'garden gun', slightly smaller bore than a .410, I was highly successful. I sat quietly on the old manger and hadn't been there more than a few minutes before a rat came scuttling across the strawed yard to the round iron feeding troughs. I waited; seconds later two more arrived, then more, and they started fighting over the few remaining drops of food. To my delight I bagged four with my first shot, and by the time I left for home half an hour later, I had fifteen tail-tips in a paperbag in my pocket – 2s 6d worth, or the equivalent of two and a half weeks' pocket-money.

One afternoon when I arrived up at Biddles it was pouring with rain. Fred greeted me cheerfully with 'A good afternoon for a bit of dentistry.'

I looked at him enquiringly. 'What?'

Fred laughed. 'Come on, slip on an apron and come with me.' We went up to the farrowing pens, where there were a number of litters of varying ages. Fred produced an instrument that looked like an oversized pair of modern-day nail clippers.

'What are you going to do?'

'Cut back the ends of the baby tusks. Piglets are born with temporary ones and they are like b****y needles. If you don't do something about it, they can lacerate a sow's udder, so I always nip the sharp ends off. It only takes seconds and saves the sows a hell of a lot of discomfort. You can catch and I'll cut, but we'll shut the mums outside. They don't take kindly to anyone upsetting their young and, personally, I'd sooner face a wicked tempered boar any day than a sow who's half-crazed thinking someone is hurting her babies'.

I was to take Fred's point quickly, for the mother of the first litter went berserk and did her utmost to get over the door at us. This was accompanied by a fierce guttural sort of bark – it was really scary, particularly when glancing round I saw that she had her forelegs over the top of the door and was displaying most of her forty-four teeth in a most unfriendly manner. The piglets, incidentally, weren't squealing because of what Fred was doing, but because they objected strongly to being caught and held. When he'd finished and the noise had abated, Fred opened the door and the agitated mum rushed in. Within seconds she was stretched out, grunting contentedly, as she wriggled into position to give her family full access to the milk bar.

'Right, now we'll go and do the major job.

I looked enquiringly at Fred 'What's that?'

'Old Prim Lad needs his tusks cutting back.

Burnham Prim Lad was the senior stock boar. Unlike many, he was as gentle as a lamb an outstanding sire and a prolific winner in the showring but however quiet a boar's tusks are lethal.

'Is that really necessary? He's so placid, he'll even take a nice gooey bit of toffee out of my hand.'

Fred laughed 'I'm sure he will. He's a real old softy, but should he ever get upset, just one sideways slash at anyone, or another pig, he'd open whichever it was to the bone. I should have done it before, but just haven't got round to it. A lot of owners don't bother, but your dad always insists on it, just in case anything should happen.'

Prim Lad's lower tusks protruded a good two and a half to three inches and, looked at from a fresh viewpoint, were undoubtedly menacing. Fred roped him in the same way as we had the store pigs a few weeks previously, passed the end of the rope through a ring cemented into the wall, pulled the boar's head up as high as possible and made the rope fast. His 'patient' didn't seem over disturbed as he, Fred, set to work with a hacksaw to cut off the offending tusks as close to the lower jaw as possible. They were about three-quarters of an inch thick where Fred was working. It seemed obvious that the tusks were not as sensitive as our teeth, for Prim Lad just stood quietly, giving the occasional little grunt and shuffling his front feet, as Fred sawed away, but I didn't like it, not one little bit. My sympathy was all with the apparently stoical boar, for it brought back vivid memories of my first visit to an aged dentist – he'd been a real butcher.

When Fred had finished removing the tusks, which I kept as souvenirs for years, he sent me across to the feedroom, where various items of equipment were stored, to collect a piece of board, mallet, chisel and some emery paper. He then proceeded to place Prim Lad's feet in turn on the board and give him a pedicure. Fred cut back the elongated ends by the simple expedient of placing the chisel on the required spot and giving it a mighty whack with the mallet. He then smoothed off the ends of the tusks and toes with the emery paper and, when satisfied with his work, released Prim Lad, who after a couple of grunts and a good shake, headed for me, snout upraised. Unlike Blaze he couldn't really nuzzle my pocket, but he did his best and left no doubt as to what he was after – toffee. Having satisfied his desire, we left the pen, Fred saying, 'That's another good job done, better safe than sorry.' I was to think of his words the following July, at the Royal Show at Newcastle.

Father always took me, from a very early age, to the Royal Show, Smithfield Show and the Dairy Show. From about fourteen I was there to help with the showing, when necessary, as well as to learn. I still have my 1935 Stockman's Ticket which

SMITHFIELD CLUB SHOW, 1935

EXHIBITOR'S SERVANT'S TICKET

Admit *M. J. Owst*

No. *450* to attend LIVE STOCK

NOT TRANSFERABLE *Leonard Frill*

*Secretary.*

N.B.—The Exhibitor's Servant must sign his name on the back of this Ticket, and show it each time he enters at the door set apart for him. He must also sign his name, if required, in the Free-List Book at that door.

[TURN OVER.

admitted me as such to Smithfield Show. At the Newcastle Royal I was on the showground the evening before the show opened. Father was attending a meeting being held there of the Sheep Breeders Council and I had time to kill whilst this was going on.

It was a glorious summer's evening and, having spent some time with Fred, I strolled along past the end of the pig-lines. As I did so I spied two mammoth Large Black boars approaching in opposite directions, one being exercised by a lad about the same age as myself. Both he and the other herdsman had showing boards and pig sticks for guiding their charges. The former were about two feet six inches high and two feet wide, with a handle in the top to carry them by. They are used to help turn pigs when showing and to slip between two pigs that come face to face, as pigs are not always friendly towards each other. I noticed both boars had massive tusks, as big as or even bigger than Prim Lad's had been. Just when they were passing each other some five yards apart, the one that the man was in charge of made a sudden run at the other, catching his herdsman completely asleep. The young lad, instead of pushing his board between the two, panicked and stuck out his knee, just as the attacker made a fierce slash at his intended victim. There was a piercing scream from the boy, as the boar's tusk neatly sliced off his kneecap, just as cleanly as though it had been done with a scalpel. All was pandemonium. The two boars tore into each other, a truly terrifying spectacle, before they were parted with boards by the various other pigmen, including Fred, who came running up. I ran to the boy and did what little I could, before his father and several helpers arrived and carried him off. Shattered as I was, I remember thinking what Fred had said about it being better to be safe than sorry and how wise Father was on insisting that tusks on all boars on the estate must be removed.

As mentioned previously, we regularly had overseas buyers coming to purchase pedigree stock. Whilst I was doing my stint at Biddles, we had several visitors, including one party from Japan headed by an industrialist whose hobby was breeding pedigree pigs. He was a Mr Mitsubishi; whether he was a forebear of the current car manufacturers I've no idea, but he certainly wasn't short of money, for he came nearly every year. The party was accompanied by an interpreter and Billy Wiltshire, a partner in the firm of Harry Hobson & Co, one of the (if not the) leading firms of pedigree livestock auctioneers. As was usually the case with such visitors they ended up at Pound Cottage for one of Mother's famous teas.

During the course of this Billy Wiltshire asked how my rabbits were doing. I bred and showed White Beverans and Flemish Giants and had been very successful with them. I told him this, going on to say that I thought I had the best young Flemish Giant buck I had ever seen and that he'd take a lot of beating at shows in the years to come. The interpreter had been doing his job. Suddenly Mr Mitsubishi clapped his hands and smiled across the table at me. It appeared that after tea he wished to see my rabbits. Full of pride, I set up the young buck on the judging table that I kept in the large shed that housed my rabbits. Rabbits, for show, have to be trained to sit quietly, ears pricked, portraying the best outline possible. To me 'my boy' looked faultless. Mr Mitsubishi asked if he could handle him and, much to my surprise, he went over the rabbit in the most professional manner.

Then there was much chat amongst our visitors and, finally, Billy Wiltshire was drawn into the conversation. He turned to me. 'Mr Mitsubishi would like to buy your young buck to take back to Japan and two does if you have them.' At that time a good show rabbit could be bought for £5 or less, but I didn't want to sell my youngster, as he was the best I'd ever bred.

'That's very nice of him, but he's not for sale and, anyway, if one sells the best of one's stock it's bad breeding policy.'

Billy Wiltshire laughed, 'You're as bad as your father.'

That afternoon Dad had refused 150 guineas (pedigree stock were always sold in guineas) for what he considered to be the best Berkshire gilt ever bred at Burnham, probably the best in the country. The offered price was about three times the true market value, but neither Mr Mitsubishi nor Billy Wiltshire could get him to change his mind. They were having the same difficulty with me. 'Come on, everything has a price.'

I didn't want to sell, so, to stop any further arguing, I decided to ask a ridiculous price. 'Oh, all right, 25 guineas and not a penny less.'

There was further talk, and then Billy turned to me: 'And what about does?'

'No problem. There's a choice of four at 10 guineas each.' The going rate was £2 to £3, and I wanted to part with two of them anyway.

Mr Mitsubishi inspected the four, selected two and again went into solemn conclave with the interpreter and Billy Wiltshire, who after a few minutes turned to me. 'Right, Mr Mitsubishi agrees the price and has asked me to arrange their shipment at the same time as his pigs. So, young Michael, as I am doing that and you have received a quite exorbitant price, I shall be charging my usual commission and you'll be paid through the firm in the normal way.'

I didn't argue. I was totally flabbergasted – 45 guineas, well, £45 when Harry Hobson & Co had taken their cut. I was rich beyond my wildest dreams. For that sort of money one could get a very nice second-hand Austin Seven or Morris Minor, with probably not more than thirty to forty thousand on the clock. Not that I was old enough to run a car, but the mere fact that I could afford one gave me a feeling of great achievement.

When the party eventually left, I received a lecture from Father about selling one's best breeding stock. Did I not realise that the Burnham flock of Hampshire Down sheep, or the two herds of pigs, had not reached the heights they had by selling off the top animals? Father was obviously cross, I was elated.

But the story didn't end there. About two weeks after Mr Mitsubishi's visit the Eton College Beagles met at Farnham Royal. Edward Clifton-Brown was an old Etonian and consequently the hounds were always welcome. Their first draw was Forty Acres, where they quickly found, their quarry taking them across Biddles Lane into Gorse Field and on straight through the pig pens, causing much running, jumping and squealing by the thirty to forty inmates. One gilt slipped and broke her back and had to be put down. It was a prime example of sod's law, as the casualty was the gilt for which Father had refused the astronomical figure of 150 guineas!

# 8

# *The Stick*

THE 1930s must have been one of the most depressed times in the history of British agriculture: farmer after farmer went broke, thousands of acres remained uncared for and land could be bought for a song. So discouraged was the farming community that this state of affairs carried on into the 1940s. I remember buying 190 acres of good 'grass' land for £17 per acre in 1941, but that's another story.

The Burnham Grove estate was not immune from the many trials and tribulations which beset agriculture in the 1930s, and milk production, in particular, was hard hit. It seemed that there was a sudden jinx on the Lynch Hill herd. Firstly one of the best milkers slipped going out of the cowshed and broke her pelvis and had to be shot. Then a heifer (one of the few which were reared on the estate, as the numbers were kept up by buying in freshly calved cows when required) got out into a one year clover ley and was dead from bloat when found. This was followed by three cows found dead in the byre over a period of a few months, two within twenty-four hours of each other and the third a couple of months later. All had died from anthrax, a deadly killer, for which there is no known cure. Further it is a so-called notifiable disease, thus involving the police. All were cows that had been on the farm for several years, so how did they become infected? Cottonseed cake, imported from Egypt, was part of their daily diet. The Ministry of Agriculture's veterinary inspector, whom Father called in when the third cow died, laid the blame at the door of the imported feeding stuff and when the use of this was discontinued all seemed to be well. The gold cup for the cleanest milk produced in the county again came to Burnham and the overall milk yield, in spite of ceasing to use cottonseed cake, went up.

Alas, this happy state of affairs was not to last long. One day, just after lunch, Jim Light arrived at the estate office, obviously very upset. Having finished his dinner he decided to take a walk through the cows, which were conveniently in a field just behind his cottage. To his horror, he found one had aborted her calf at between six and seven months into her pregnancy. Contagious abortion was probably the most dreaded disease amongst dairy farmers, more so even than foot and mouth. At least with the latter all were slaughtered and the government paid compensation at the full market value. Contagious abortion could decimate a herd and negate a farmer's livelihood.

Dad phoned Aubrey Ward, the vet. He'd just come in and was about to have something to eat, but promised to be at Lynch Hill within the hour. He took the aborted calf to send away to have tests done and said the cow should be isolated, which, in fact, had already been done. There was no known cure for contagious abortion, although *Thompson's Elementary Veterinary Science*, originally published in 1895, reads: 'This malady has been known from time immemorial, reference being made to it in Biblical history, for, according to Genesis 31:38, Jacob seems to have known the secret of prevention, it is, therefore, a great pity he did not leave it behind him for our benefit in these latter days.'

Four days later the worst was known: it was confirmed as contagious abortion. I seldom ever remember seeing Father so downhearted. Farming is fraught with worries and disappointments, but this, with times already bad, was really one below the belt. Two days later another cow slipped her calf. Jim Light, whilst obviously shattered by events, remained reasonably optimistic and assured Father that he knew two certain remedies which would avert any further cases. Father asked what he had in mind. Jim explained that the first was given to him by his grandfather who, in turn, had been told it by his grandfather, so it dated well back into the eighteenth century. Apparently the aborted calf and afterbirth had to be burned to ash; then this was spread on the floor at the entrance of the byre, so that the cows walked over it as they came in and out for milking. Jim said he'd seen it done as a boy when it had been one hundred per cent successful – it couldn't fail. Father gave his consent and enquired what Jim's second solution might be.

'Buy a billy goat. You'll never get cows aborting if you run an old billy or two with them.' This was a well-known and popular belief. In the dairying areas it was almost a rule, rather than the exception, to see billy goats with every herd.

'Right, Jim, you go ahead with your ash idea and I'll get hold of a couple of goats. I'll be honest – I haven't much faith in either, but under the circumstances, we may as well try everything we can.' That evening I heard Father telling Mother that he thought Jim's 'burnt offering' smacked strongly of witchcraft, but, what the hell, sometimes these old cures, passed down from generation to generation, worked.

The following Thursday I went off with Harry Jaycock, the driver of the estate lorry, to Bracknell market. I had two pounds in my pocket and instructions to buy two billies. It was always a good market for goats. This day was no exception and there were ten for sale – seven nannies and three billies, all with big sweeping horns and all stinking to high heaven. Few animals, anyway to me, smell worse than a billy goat. I'm told, but have never attempted to verify this, it is because they urinate on their beards. Whatever the reason, with the possible exception of a few pampered show specimens, they stink!

Having inspected the three, none of whom seemed very friendly and one of whom was downright aggressive, I seated myself on the edge of one of the pens to await the auctioneer, who was selling the sheep at the far end of the line. One could buy a nice young nanny that hadn't had a kid at anything from half a crown (2s 6d) to seven shillings and sixpence, so I estimated a billy, at the most, wouldn't cost more than five bob. At last the auctioneer reached where Harry and I waited.

'Right, now gentlemen, the goats, we've a fine selection today. First, lot 117, an eighteen-month-old billy, guaranteed quiet and fertile. Who'll start me at £1.' There was silence. 'Well, ten bob then? Come along, gentlemen, we haven't got all day.'

An elderly gypsy-looking man raised his hand, 'Two bob.'

'Two shillings I'm bid, two shillings, any advance on two?'

I wanted to get home for lunch, so I raised my hand, 'Five bob'.

'A crown I'm bid. Any advance on a crown?' It didn't seem as though there was going to be until the auctioneer said, 'For the last time . . .' At that an elderly lady, clad in a dress that looked as though it could have done service in the reign of Queen Victoria, her head adorned with a much-flowered hat and strong pebble glasses perched on her nose, prodded at the auctioneer with her umbrella, 'Ten shillings.' Blast! I bid another half crown, but immediately there was another wave of the brolly. 'Fifteen.' I dropped out, as the pace was getting too hot!

I bought the two remaining billies at five shillings each, which meant I'd got the aggressive one, but I didn't give it much thought at the time. I went to the office and paid; then Harry and I half-led, half-pulled my purchases over to the lorry and he lifted them in, spitting and hawking as he did so.

'Phew, the b*****s don't half stink. No wonder you don't get abortion with them around. Reckon I'll have to wash the lorry out when I get back.'

We found Jim and, on his instructions, let the billies straight out with the cows. They must have known each other, for they made no attempt to fight, nor did they pay any attention to the cows. Later that afternoon I called in at Lynch Hill to give a hand with the milking and was quickly told I'd bought a right so-and-so, but that wasn't exactly the terminology used. Apparently, when Ken Light had gone to bring the cows in for afternoon milking, the billy that had shown animosity at the mart charged him. Fortunately Ken had a stick with him and a few quick whacks sent the billy away in a hurry, but the general opinion was that he was no friendly old goat as often portrayed in children's books in those days.

About ten days later I met Bob Hedges and George Devonshire one evening at the end of Bangle's Spinney. Both seemed in high good humour. It was George who spoke first. 'You should have been with us three-quarters of an hour ago. You missed a real pantomime, haven't laughed so much for years.'

Bob, a broad grin spreading across his face, took up the story. 'We had a grandstand view. We were 'cocked up' by the big oak at the bottom of Lynch Hill field, watching out for any of our poaching friends, when I looked round just in time to see Mrs Clifton-Brown and her old Sandy getting over the stile out of Lammas Wood.' Sandy was a nasty snappy little Cairn Terrier, who seemed to hate everyone, baring his mistress. 'She starts walking along the side of the wood towards Hay hill. The cows were on the other side of the stream with, of course, the goats. Anyway, she was about halfway to the gate into Hay Mill meadow when the big billy, the nasty one, sees her and Sandy and, it seemed, she sees him. Anyway she starts to hurry.'

George, laughing heartily, cut in and took up the story again. 'The billy he sets off at a brisk trot back towards the watersplash, to cross the stream by the wood, and the missus, well I don't think she liked what she saw, for she changed up into a higher gear and steps out faster than I've ever seen her move before, looking back over her shoulder all the time. Once he'd crossed the stream, old billy boy speeded up too and was obviously gaining.

When madam realised this she dropped her stick, hoisted her skirt with both hands and made a sprint for the gate, her bright pink bloomers making a right show. I've heard of a red rag to a bull; I reckon pink bloomers must have the same effect on a billy, for he really motored. She was over that gate like a sixteen-year-old lad and landed on her backside just as the billy hit the gate. I know it might have been serious, but we were too far away to help, but laugh, I nearly cried.'

'What did you do?' I looked enquiringly at the two men. It was Bob who answered.

'We nipped across the plank bridge, at the teal pond. When we got through the wire, that flipping goat thought it would have a go at us, but George soon changed its mind. He fired into the ground, just in front of it, as it was charging at us. That stopped it and it took off at the rate of knots.' George laughed.

'Yes, and if the old lady hadn't been there, when it had got far enough away, I'd have given it the second barrel up its backside, and stung it up a bit. Instead, we ran across to the missus, helped her up, collected her stick and saw her safely back into the wood where she couldn't meet up with the goat again. But laugh, if only you could have seen her sprinting for the gate. I never thought she could have moved so fast, but there, I suppose a charging goat could be a great spur.'

Later that evening Father received a very testy phone call from E. C. B. to the effect that the vicious goat must be got rid of at once. Next day was Slough market and a protesting Harry Jaycock took the offending animal into the mart. He returned to say it had been bought by the gipsy-looking man who'd been at Bracknell for two shillings – a maiden bid.

Regretably, neither goats nor ashes had any useful effect, as three more cows aborted in the course of the next few weeks. Father, who always told me that 'the first loss was the least loss', recommended to Edward Clifton-Brown that the herd and the small number of heifers being brought on as replacements should be agglutination tested (this blood test shows whether an animal is infected with contagious abortion or not) and that those that passed should be sold as dairy cows. Those that failed the test should be dried off and fattened for the butcher. More than three-quarters of the herd passed the test and a reasonably successful dispersal sale was quickly held.

Farming is very much, or was, a matter of ups and downs. It was a sad day for me when the herd went, very much a down, but it quickly brought forth an up. It was decided that Lynch Hill should become a beef producing unit, the breed favoured being Devons – not the great big South Devons, or South Hams as they were frequently known, but the Red Rubies from North Devon and West Somerset. Quite a number were already 'finished' each summer on Lees Farm, the north-east section of the estate. This farm was basically free-range poultry, but there was always a lot of excellent grazing following where the hens had been and the fattened bullocks were much sought after by the local butchers. Father bought them, almost entirely, from one 'Varmer Sam' Locke of South Molton on the edge of Exmoor. A wonderful character, he had the broadest of Devon accents, with such a pronounced burr that even Father, who came from the West Country, at times had difficulty in following him. He was one of the straightest men I have ever met and a lovely personality. Whilst retired from serious farming and cattle dealing, he still had land in various places around the area, which he kept stocked with carefully selected bullocks. He was a shrewd and knowledgeable judge of cattle and a hard nut to do a deal with. He was, also, the licensee of a small pub, 'The Ring o' Bells', and it was there where deals were finalised over a drink.

In the early autumn, after the Lynch Hill herd was dispersed, it was agreed with E. C. B. that Father should set about buying 75 to 100 bullocks to fill the yards and cow byre at the farm. Jim Light had left, although he could have stayed to look after the beef cattle, but, as he said, he was first and foremost a cowman. George Claridge, another of the herdsmen, went with him to his new job. Ken Light, whose hobby had been carpentry and very good he was too, joined Charlie Davis and Alf Small in the estate workshop, helping do everything from building hay wagons to the repair and maintenance of the estate cottages and farm buildings.

It was now almost automatic that I accompanied Father on such trips and this was no exception. We motored down to Devon, a day's journey, and stayed at Appledore with my grandmother. We were with 'Varmer Sam', as everyone called him, by 10.00 a.m. the following day. After Dad had assured him that the last thing he needed, so early in the morning, was a large whisky, we got in the car and drove up to some land 'Varmer Sam' had at Molland, on Exmoor. When we reached there Father turned to me and said, 'Right, you pick out what we want and you and Mr

Locke can make the price. I shan't interfere unless you're going hopelessly wrong.'

Father and old Sam stayed by the gate, chatting, as I walked out across the field. There was a large stone, thatched linhay (shed) in the far corner and the high Devon banks gave great shelter against the wind. I counted eighteen bullocks spread out across the field. They looked sleek and well except for three I didn't care for. Two were leggy and definitely had some South Ham in them and one, a good deal smaller than the rest, didn't match. The remainder were quality forward stores, each weighing between 7½ to 8 hundredweight. I walked back to the gate, told 'Varmer Sam' I was discarding three and asked the price. Because I was dropping three, he said he couldn't take less than £20 a head, I walked back through them again this time with Father who said nothing. One I noticed was a potential show bullock. We rejoined their owner.

'Right, £16 and not a penny more.' Then followed ten minutes of haggling, 'Varmer Sam' extolling the merits of his bullocks, whilst I said, rightly, that they'd lose between a quarter and a half a hundredweight by the time they'd made the train journey up to Burnham. Eventually we agreed a price – £17 10s per head.

Father never said a word until 'Varmer Sam' and I smacked hands, the old traditional way of clinching a deal. 'Well done, you've got them at ten shillings a head less than I'd have gone to. You better carry on and buy the rest.'

Sam Locke put his hand on my shoulder and said, 'You obviously know a good beast when you see one and you're fair, that's important. Always remember the seller has to make a living as well as the buyer and you'll find, if you're straight with people, they'll normally be straight with you.' I wish I could have written his words in the vernacular, but I haven't the ability and, if I had, few would understand it anyway. Over the years I have always tried to remember his advice, which, I think, has been to the advantage of all concerned.

By lunchtime we had bought 45 head. We went back to 'The Ring o' Bells', where 'Varmer Sam' put on his other hat and dispensed drinks. He insisted I should have a port and lemon – I thought it was horrible! When arrangements had been made about railing the cattle up to Burnham, Sam left the room. He came back a few minutes later carrying a hazel thumb-stick, which I noticed he'd been using in the morning. He presented it to me and then told me its history. When he was eight years old he had accompanied his father for the first time to a cattle fair, the Spring Fair at Molland. Close to where we had gone that morning, his father had stopped and cut the stick out of the hedge and presented it to young Sam – that had been in 1871. Now, he said, it was time for it to move on – move on to someone who loved and understood cattle. He continued that, after what he'd seen and heard that morning, I was that someone. I protested that I couldn't possibly accept what had virtually become a Locke family heirloom, but he insisted, telling me to care for it and, if I did, it would, in turn, care for me.

Over the years that followed I bought and sold, quite literally, thousands of store and beef cattle and, when I remembered, which was usually, I took the stick with me. I can never, knowingly, remember making a bad deal. Now 123 years after it was cut out of a hedge on the road to Molland, I have no further use for it and have passed it on to my daughter. She's unlikely to go buying cattle, but who knows? She has a few acres of land and one day, perhaps, she might just want a bullock or two to graze it. If she does I hope she takes 'The Stick' with her and it passes on the wisdom of 'Varmer Sam'. One thing I do know is that she won't buy a 7½ to 8 hundredweight bullock for £17 10s, which would hardly buy a decent joint of beef these days!

# 9

# 'Still a Babbee'

I often wonder, these days, whether farmers and, indeed, the limited number of men they employ, have the same love and feel for the land as they did in the 1920s, 1930s and before. The conclusion I have reached, perhaps wrongly, is that they can't have, they just haven't the time, for modern farming seems to be all rush and tear. Vast tractors, ploughs, combines, sprayers, all cover acres and acres in a day, the operators in comfortable cabs, often with radios, air conditioning, heaters, even computers – high above the ground they're working. There seems to be nothing personal, no contact, not as one had when following a pair of horses all day, then attending to their welfare before seeing to one's own after knocking off in the evening. To me, land has now become, in many many instances, a medium in which seed is placed, the right chemical formula worked out and applied, to be followed by a series of 'inoculations' to the crop as sprayers race up and down the fields, on well-defined tracks, immunising it against a host of maladies. Rich land and poor land are outdated terms, for whilst the texture of the soil will vary, the fertility is now largely a question of applying a sufficient amount of the right chemicals.

Gone are the days when one would hear such remarks as, 'That be a right good field to fatten a bullock, always has been' or 'That be grand land to finish heifers, but ain't no good for bullocks.' I remember once when carting wheat in Nobb's Crook and I was on the rick forking the sheaves to 'Gunner' Stingmore, the builder. He turned te me as we 'topped off' and remarked 'Gran' ole field this, bain't a better un for wheat for miles aroun'.' Such comments are history for a field these days is as good as the fertiliser spreader makes it, as output is the key word. This undoubtedly has to be in the world that evolved. Whether it is for the good and betterment of the human race only time will tell, but it seems unlikely when thousands of acres, although I suppose I should now say hectares, of good cropable land stand idle each year, due to over-production, whilst millions throughout the world are on the verge of starvation. One thing is certain: much has been removed from our countryside which will never return however hard the environmentalists may try.

In pre-war days almost every operation in farming was an 'event'. There was week upon week of ploughing laboriously pulling acres and acres of mangolds or picking potatoes behind a spinner. Much of the latter was piecework done by gangs of women. I remember one girl in her early twenties who came 'spud picking' for several years. She was an absolute wizard and would earn a pound or more in a week than any other member of the gang. She was about four feet eight inches and claimed her success was due to the fact that she was small in stature and thus nearer to the ground. Picking 'taties' was a serious but light-hearted occasion, with much chat, raucous singing and plenty of ribald and risqué comments to Tom Rose, when he came to check their work. Tom didn't like potato lifting time. He found the ladies hard-going, and he eventually told Father it had to be a choice between him or them. From then on the gang was made up of men and boys.

The main 'events' were, of course, haymaking and harvesting. Frequently these took on the air of a party, for tea in the hayfield was often akin to a picnic, but I can assure readers that haymaking was far from being one. Anyone who has pitched hay up onto a wagon all the afternoon on a hot summer's day will need no convincing. Even worse was loading a wagon with a hayloader attached to the back, gathering up the crop and dropping it, almost literally, onto the men, usually two, who valiantly coped with the steady flow that rained down upon them. The loading of the wagon had to be precise, for if not it would slip and fall off on the way to the rick. One got no marks for that!

When tea time came it provided a much-needed breather. The gang would gather at some central point and seat themselves gratefully on the ground, for a well-earned rest. Tea was provided by the 'farmer' and at Burnham it would be prepared by the wife of one of the men living on the estate, for which, of course, she was paid. The actual tea would be brought out to the field in one, or sometimes two, white enamelled buckets with covers (in reality the slop pails found in any bedroom where there was a washstand, with its matching wash basin, cold water jug, etcetera). In addition to the actual tea there would be a seemingly mammoth supply of sandwiches. It was no small task making these, for there was no such thing as sliced bread in those days, and the team of anything up to a dozen men would expect to be able to satisfy their hunger. The filling was normally strawberry or raspberry jam, although a much-appreciated alternative was Lyle's Golden Syrup. Frequently children would join the party and help hand out mugs of tea, whilst quietly nicking the occasional sandwich, particularly if the filling happened to be syrup.

Half an hour was the usual break and when thirst and hunger had been satiated it was time to relax and chat. Sometimes one of the older hands would start, 'I mind back in the '80s [1880s]' and some old yarn would be recounted, probably for the umpteenth time. The best storytellers were old Bill Herbert and 'Gunner' Stingmore. As a child I would sit, goggle-eyed, as he told of skirmishes with the Boers in the blazing heat of the veldt. 'Gunner' had great respect for the Boers, said they were brave and fearless fighters, but claimed they were dirty devils who never washed a dish, or plate, after a meal, but instead just let the dogs lick them clean. Of course I and the other youngsters believed every word.

Similar tea breaks occurred at harvest time, the only difference being that even more staff were involved. Occasionally, when a real drive was being made of an evening to finish a field and get all the sheaves gathered in before the weather broke, Father would arrive with two or three gallons of beer in a churn and every man received a pint. The builder, for some reason I never really discovered, got two. Certainly he was the key man in the whole rick building operation. He was the one who gave symmetry and uniformity to the structure of the stack, making it something to be proud of, and it was he who controlled the speed at which it went up. It was no good having wagons loaded high if there was a hold-up at the rick. Whilst the builder had to be fast, he had to lay the sheaves correctly so the rick was safe and would not move. Otherwise, at the worst, the whole lot could slide over into a heap, and at the best 'policemen' would be required – great baulks of timber rammed into the side of the rick to stop it from collapsing. For such a thing to happen was a terrible stigma on the builder and something which took years to live down – particularly if it happened after he'd had his ration of beer! Fortunately I can never remember it happening at Burnham, the worst I can recall being a lone 'policeman' holding up the corner of a rick. Such a pick-me-up as a pint of beer was greatly appreciated and certainly was not a time waster, for, after a hard day's harvesting, the life span of a pint, when it reached the hands of a sweating, thirsty man, could be measured in seconds rather than minutes.

I still well remember the degradation and shame that resulted from my first pint in the harvest field. The weather had been appalling, and one hoped and prayed from day to day for an improvement.

Back in the 1930s the forecasts issued by the meteorological office were frequently far from accurate, many seeming to be not much more than a calculated guess, so, often it paid to heed the old and trusted indications and country maxims. Cows standing in a pond, or river, were said to be a sign of good weather to come. Conversely, if they were all lying down it was an indication of rain. Swallows, swifts and house martins flying high were a guarantee of a fine day. This, over many years, I have found to be remarkably accurate. Equally, if one kept hearing the rather attractive laughter-like call of the green woodpecker, it was a forewarning of rain. Seldom was this shy and wily bird wrong. Like so many of our birds it has local names. In certain parts it is known as a 'rain-bird', in other districts as a 'rain-fowl'.

Mind you, sunshine didn't always mean a grand day for farmers. Many a time on a soaking wet morning I was greeted by one of the older hands with 'Marnin, gran' day, gert drop o' rain, t'will do a power o' good. Us needed un bad.' There was one lovely old character who came annually, for a number of years, to take on hoeing piecework. His nickname was 'Throstle', an old country name for a songthrush, although I never heard him break into song. He would invariably greet one with, 'Marnin, nice marnin an' if 'tis as nice a marnin termorrer marnin as 'tis this marnin, it'll be a nice marnin.' Should it be raining he would substitute 'b\*\*\*\*y wet marnin' for 'nice marnin'. A much-respected pundit on the subject of the weather was 'Gunner' Stingmore. He claimed that if the wind followed the sun round, then one could be sure of a fine day. If it didn't, watch out, as it would be raining by nightfall. He was seldom wrong.

When the weather eventually took up, to use a nautical term, it was a case of all hands to the pumps. We were carting barley from the big field at the back of Lynch Hill Farm, and because there were two separate gangs carting and one stooking sheaves behind the binder, as the last field was being cut, everyone was needed and I was entrusted with a wagon, pulled by Sprey, a magnificent Suffolk Punch mare. This meant I had to build the load on the wagon in the field, as the sheaves were pitched to me, then take it to the farm and fork the sheaves to a man on the rick. As the latter grew, so this task became more demanding. We'd just started to fill my wagon, when one of the carters arrived back for another load and brought a bucket of beer with him. I jumped down to the ground, as Jack Adaway took charge of the bucket and tankards, appointing himself chief dispenser of our bounty. Being sixteen, I was allowed by Father to have a half. Jack passed me a full tankard. I took it rather gingerly, for I was used to doing what I was told and I'd only ever drunk mild – this was best bitter. I raised my glass, 'Cheers', and then made the mistake of trying to keep up with my companions – they seemed to just open their throats and pour. However, choking slightly, I finished as Jack looked in the tea bucket. 'Ah, be a mite left, hold your mugs out, lads.' There was no doubt it was good stuff, but when Jack got to me I shook my head. 'No thanks, I've had enough.'

'Go on, boy. Be you man or babbee?'

I felt good. I held out my tankard. A few minutes later I climbed back onto the wagon. 'Froggy' Hawkins, one of the pitchers, took Sprey by the bridle and led her forward between two rows of stooks. Sheaves seemed to be flying up from all directions. I was half buried as I struggled to build the load. My face felt flushed and I was streaming sweat as I endeavoured to lay the sheaves in order to finish with a safe load.

'Right, that's enough.' I looked over the edge at the men below.

'No, reckon you'm can take another round or two, or don't 'ee think you can build un?' I felt hot, but good. I looked down at Jack.

'Of course I can. Easy.'

'Well, let's see 'ee then.' The sheaves came winging up. Five minutes later, I shouted down that that was enough – no more. 'Froggy' stood back and scratched his head as he surveyed the load.

'Reckon 'er's as skew-whiff as a dog's 'ind leg. You'm should rope 'er.' I peered over the edge of the load; it was high.

'No, it'll be as safe as houses. Pass the end of the reins up with your fork. I may as well ride up here. Save time when I get to the rick.'

'Froggy' did as I asked, but as I reached out for the end of the reins, I saw him give a sly wink to Jack as he said,

"Im's the boss's son, reckon, with all 'is edication, 'e'd know more 'an us ole boys.'

I paid no attention as I settled down, my legs hanging over the front of the load. Sprey plodded across the field, throwing her weight into the collar. I could feel the sheaves of corn under me swaying a bit, but why not? It was by far the biggest load to be brought in for the day and I'd built it and I'd had a pint and a half of bitter – it was great stuff, more bite in it than mild. I'd drink that in future, even if it did cost sixpence a pint; it would be worth it. As I approached the gate an empty wagon pulled into the field. It was Charlie Hawkins, the head horseman at Britwell (no relation to 'Froggy'). Boxer was between the shafts. He and Sprey normally worked as a pair. Charlie pulled Boxer to a halt.

'What in hell's name be you doing up there, Mr Michael? You should know better 'n that. Particarly the way uns leaning, danged unsafe it look an' no rope neither, right daft.'

I waved nonchalantly. 'Don't worry, it'll be okay.' I shook the reins and Sprey moved on towards the gate. As I proceeded to guide her through, I realised I couldn't see the gateposts, and it was tricky enough when one could. Suddenly there was a grinding crunch as the rear-wheel hub caught the right-hand post. The wagon lurched drunkenly and the entire load slid into the lane, nearly burying me as it did so. I struggled free and clambered over the pile of sheaves to get to Sprey, but she wasn't panicking; she just stood quietly, helping herself from a sheaf that had come within her reach.

The men, both on the rick and in the field, had seen what had happened and were making their way in my direction, but it could not be said that they were hurrying to my assistance. Until they arrived, 'operation harvest' was at a standstill, for the slipped load had completely closed the lane and opening to the field. Charlie Hawkins turned his wagon and came back. When he reached me he shook his head, 'I told 'ee, but you knew best, but reckon you'll larn.' As soon as I could I backed Sprey into the field, jumped up into the wagon as, silently, the sheaves were pitched up to me. The same was happening with Charlie.

When all was cleared up I slid down to the ground and mumbled 'Sorry'. Old Jack Adaway put his hand on my shoulder, 'An, so you b****y well should be. Yourn a great chap when you's rattlin' the hay into us with that danged sweep, near burying us, so we gived you some o' you're own medcine this evenin' an' I reckon youm larned a mite terday.' As he and 'Froggy' turned and walked back down the field, I heard 'Froggy' say, 'Reckon 'im's still a babbee arter all, but we'll edicate 'im, 'e'll larn, e'll larn'. And I did. Truly a case of pride coming before a fall. It had been a sobering experience, in every sense of the word, as well as being extremely humiliating.

# 10

# Shows and Showing

I grew up in an environment that was highly competitive. Whether it was to produce the biggest and most shapely mangold-wurzels to exhibit at the South Bucks Ploughing Match; sweet peas at the local flower show; bantams and pigeons at the National Poultry Show; or Hampshire Down sheep at the Royal or Smithfield Fatstock Show, there was only one aim – namely to win. Seconds and thirds were all right, but really no more than a spur to do better next time. Of course one didn't always win, not by any manner of means, for there were many others with a similar philosophy. The competition was intense, but, broadly speaking, the rivalry was normally friendly and good-natured, at least at the agricultural shows, but it could hot up, to say the least, at local events. At the former the main objective and, indeed, the focal point of the show was the livestock. In those days, machinery and trade stands were secondary to the animals. I cannot remember there being a tractor or any piece of equipment on display at the first Smithfield Show I attended, at the Agricultural Hall in Islington, in the late 1920s. There probably was, tucked away in some remote corner, but, unlike today it wasn't what the show was all about.

As the years have passed, more and more emphasis has been given to stands, whilst the overall livestock entry has decreased, as has the number of breeds, many that were shown in large numbers now being classified as 'rare breeds'. But memories remain of the parades of prize-winning cattle at the Royal, Bath and West and other major shows in the 1920s and 1930s, when they quite literally filled the main ring – magnificent animals, exhibited with pride, as indeed they are today, and representing hours of dedicated work by the stockmen. The sentiment remains the same, but the numbers and breeds have changed dramatically.

The correct presentation of exhibits, whatever they are, is paramount. Few can be more exacting than trimming and preparing the Down breeds of sheep for show. Hours and hours would be spent carefully 'sculpting' the Hampshire Downs, as must be done today. This was a backbreaking job, as one was bent double most of the time, first levelling the back and generally shaping the sheep. After the initial heavyish cut, it was a case of carding up the wool and trimming it off with shears, over and over again, until perfectly smooth, symmetrical and as level as a billiard table. To achieve this required great skill, and Harry Wadman, the head shepherd at Burnham, and his son, Philip, were masters of the art. I spent many hours trying to learn and, eventually, could do a passable job, but, in football parlance, whilst the Wadmans were well up in the Premier League, I was struggling away down in the Third Division.

All showing, whatever it might be, takes time and dedication to be successful. I was very involved in 'The Fancy', the breeding and showing of rabbits, poultry and pigeons. It was, in pre-war days, a very popular form of recreation. Nearly every village or group of villages had a Flower Show; many also staged what was referred to as a Poultry Show, but which contained not only poultry, including bantams, but rabbits and pigeons as well.

Burnham Flower Show, held during the 1930s in Priory Meadow, was a major annual event, much looked forward to by many of the locals. There were classes for almost everyone and everything. In addition to the horticultural and poultry section, there was a large section run by the WI, which scheduled many and varied classes for bread, cakes, jam, flower arrangements, needlework and other forms of handicraft. A big attraction, for both young and old, was the fair, which was set up adjoining the show. Nothing very fancy, for vast funfairs and amusement parks were still a thing of the future. The centre piece was the merry-go-round, with its gaily painted horses, swing boats, coconut shies, a slide for the kids, a shooting gallery, hoop-la and, of course, a fortune teller, the latter being well patronised by the teenagers. Last, but by no means certainly least, was the beer tent.

The fair kept going during the evening, long after the show had closed and the exhibits had been taken home, or, as in some cases in the vegetable section, sold. If the weather was fine, a sectional wooden floor would be laid on the grass to supply the facility for dancing to a local band. Lighting was provided by a generator, run by a massive and immaculately maintained steam engine with highly polished brass and gleaming paintwork. True lords of the roads, these steam engines trundled around the country moving the funfair from one venue to another. If it was a nice warm evening, which it usually seemed to be, the older generation provided solid support for the beer tent and, whilst supping their pints, the elders would give a running and often bawdy commentary on the antics of the youngsters who pranced around the few square yards of 'floor'. Such festivity ended at ten o'clock and Priory Meadow would be left to the owls and other residents, virtually undisturbed, for another year.

I remember once, a few days after the show, being with Bob Hedges and stopping in Crow Piece Lane for a chat with old Bill Herbert. Bob asked how he'd enjoyed the Flower Show. Bill spat, looked thoughtful for a moment and then replied. 'Middlin', middlin'. Beer 't weren't bad, but I tell 'ee what, them young uns dancin', the antics they get up to nowadays, reckon there be more bones made than broke Flower Show night.' He gave a wry chuckle, spat on his hands, picked up his hook and hank and continued cutting back the grass and nettles that grew along the side of the lane.

It was in the cottagers' and allotment holders' classes that the competition really hotted up and the judges' verdicts were subject to the most detailed criticism, often not over-complimentary to either their knowledge, or, indeed, breeding. If an estate cottage did not have a large garden, its tenant was given an allotment, and five of these allotments were just beyond the Pound Cottage boundary, adjoining the lane. All allotment holders grew most of their year's supply of vegetables, several working hard to have prize-winning exhibits for the show in July, which had a number of restricted classes, even one for the largest marrow.

What is it about the humble marrow that arouses such fervour? Some growers become paranoid over potatoes, or blinded as to the brilliance of their beetroot, but they aren't in the same league as marrow growers. Setting out to grow and exhibit the largest marrow can turn a normally placid person into an obsessive, scheming rogue. Such things did happen, and at Burnham.

Fred Simpson had one of the allotments adjoining Pound Cottage. He wasn't an avid gardener, as he just grew what he needed for the table. One evening Father walked down to the allotments and asked the five occupiers, who were all busily working their plots, if they'd like any marrow plants. All said yes and Fred immediately set about making a bed – he was very partial to marrow and ginger jam. There was a large supply of well-rotted farmyard manure available and Fred concocted a bed that, once the seedlings were established, was guaranteed to nearly blow them out of the ground and produce giants. This was certainly not the original intention; he just wanted some good marrows for jam making.

After the plants had flowered and the first fruits started to form, Fred nipped off the majority of these, leaving seven or eight. As they grew he gathered up buckets of liquid manure from his charges at Britwell, took them to his allotment and lavishly fed his marrows. They grew and grew and I regularly went to view their progress; one in particular seemed to be easily outstripping the others. I persuaded Father to come and look – he was impressed. He told Fred he really should enter it for the Flower Show. Fred wasn't enthusiastic: he wasn't even keen on showing cattle, his main interest being the milk yields of his charges. However, after a little persuasion from both Dad and me, he agreed.

The growth of the marrow was carefully monitored by myself and Harry Jaycock, who had the adjoining allotment. It was probably through Harry that rumours began to circulate about the monster marrow that Fred Simpson was growing. All of a sudden there was something attractive about Pound Cottage lane. Known gardening enthusiasts, never normally seen there, had taken to having an evening stroll along past the allotments, one had to assume in the hopes of getting a glimpse of the much-vaunted marrow. One evening Harry went into his favourite pub for a pint and was warmly greeted by a man he seldom had much to do with. The latter insisted on buying and then started to pump Harry about Fred's marrow. Harry, ever a joker, extolled the vastness of the marrow, and happily agreed to measure it and report back.

A week before the show there was quite a gathering at the pub. Harry told me he was deliberately late, and when he walked in he was greeted with a chorus of 'Well?' As he went to buy a pint, two people tried to forestall him, but he managed a swallow before speaking. 'I measured it.' He hadn't, as he'd been away most of the week at an agricultural show. He took another swig of beer. 'It's three feet eleven inches long and forty-one inches in girth.' There were, Harry said, gasps of amazement and well there might have been, for Harry had grossly exaggerated.

Regrettably we were never to learn how close the marrow might have got to Harry's wildly enlarged dimensions, for early the following week, when Fred went to spend the evening in his allotment, he found his giant marrow had been cut in half with a spade. Worse, however, was the fact that all Harry's marrows had been chopped up into little pieces. Affixed to one bit, with an old nail, was a scrawled message on the inside of an empty Players cigarette packet. The writing was so bad that it was quite difficult to decipher. It read, 'Thistle teach yer ter blody lie.'

Father phoned Sergeant Garett at Burnham police station, who came round on his bike. He viewed the scene of the crime, chatted to both Harry and Fred and then retired to the estate office, to review the situation over a bottle of beer. As he truly said, there was not much useful evidence. The perpetrator was obviously very illiterate (we had a good laugh over 'thistle'), might or might not smoke Players and, presumably, had an interest in showing marrows. Not, the Sergeant decided, a lot to go on. After another bottle of beer, the case, for all intents and purposes, was closed. Fred was the least concerned of anyone. Showing just wasn't his forte, except for the support he gave me in preparing cattle for the Christmas fatstock shows.

Not long before the incident of the marrow, my Dexter cow, Whitewyck Gamet, produced her second calf. To my great disappointment, like her first, it was a bull, but what a calf. I begged Father to be allowed to keep it and run it on to show at Smithfield, where there were breed classes. Father asked E. C. B., who happily agreed and suggested that, as I was so keen, I might also like to 'do' one or two of the cattle bought for fattening for the local Christmas fatstock shows. I greeted this suggestion with great enthusiasm, picking out two of the superb Devon bullocks which had recently arrived from 'Varmer Sam' Locke and were grazing at the Lees Farm. They were good forward stores, just right to make a start on and were quickly moved to two spacious loose boxes at Britwell, together with a very nice Aberdeen Angus heifer. I really went to work on these, first teaching them to lead, then to show correctly, later, as we drew nearer the shows, bathing and grooming them, until they shone like freshly minted coins. I made up their ration and did all the feeding. Britwell being less than five minutes by bike from my home, it was easy for me to attend to them before I went off to my studies and I was back in time to tend them in the afternoon.

I remember it was a very hectic autumn, for not only had I the show cattle to attend to, but I was preparing my first exhibits for the National Poultry Show at Olympia, in conjunction with the Dairy Show. Readers may think that to show a pigeon, or a bantam, one just catches it up, takes it to the show and sticks it in a pen – wrong. If one did that they'd flutter about, break feathers and wouldn't show. I had a shed, an old eight foot by four foot hen house I'd bought at a farm sale for five shillings. With the aid of Father I built a wooden base to raise it up so I could stand comfortably and fitted it out with a tier of show pens. Of an evening I would introduce both pigeons and bantams to these, getting them quiet and accustoming them to being penned and handled. Then came the next stage, persuading them to show to full advantage. This is done with the aid of a judging stick, a telescopic metal rod, like a miniature car aerial, and one virtually tickles them under the chin, teaching them to stand correctly, or, if they squat, giving a tickle at the other end to make them stand up. They learn remarkably quickly. If this sounds ridiculous, even laughable, it is nonetheless necessary, as presentation is most important.

At last the big day came and my exhibits went off to Olympia: two Pekin bantams, a Modern Game bantam and two Racing Homers, one of which, a cock, was a prolific winner locally, so I had high hopes of a major success. The first day of the show was spent watching numbers of truly impressive cows and heifers being judged. My favourite breeds were the Dairy Shorthorns, in those days the leading dairy breed, and Jerseys. In the years to follow I was to manage highly successful herds of both, and much of that success I attribute to hours spent watching the judging at the Dairy Show and other major events, over a number of years, developing an eye. When judging and lunch were over, I would go off around the stands, having arranged to meet Father at the one that produced the *Dairy Farmer*. That and *Fur & Feather* were my favourite reading. But that day, even with so much to interest me, my mind kept straying to the first floor where the poultry show was held wondering how my exhibits were doing.

This section was not open to the public, on the first day, whilst judging was taking place.

We were at the show early the following morning. I was terribly keyed-up, for, although I was a seasoned compaigner at local shows, this was my first venture into the big time. Father had warned me not to be disappointed if I had no success, just write it off to experience. I had a catalogue and a list of my numbers and raced along the seemingly never-ending lines of pens in the poultry section until I found one of my entries – the Modern Game bantam, a pullet. I couldn t believe my eyes, for there, securely affixed to the pen, was a red card – first prize. I was ecstatic, as it was beyond my wildest dreams. I remember I was third with a black Pekin hen, but nothing with my pigeons, not even a very highly commended. I was, to say the least, somewhat despondent over this. However, it turned out to be my lucky day, for I met the judge. I've long since forgotten his name, but I do remember he was a Yorkshireman and a recognised leading authority on many breeds of pigeons. He was most gracious and, when I hinted at my disappointment, took great pains to explain his judging and gave me no end of helpful tips on breeding and loft management. As we parted he said, 'I've a four-year-old cock bird that I've finished with. If you like you can have him.' I jumped at the opportunity. Two weeks later the pigeon arrived and two years later I won first prize in a class of around a hundred Racing Homers at Olympia. At the same show I also won the medal for the best Modern Game bantam.

Smithfield was the show that seemed to generate the most excitement, at least in the sheep section. This was divided into three groups, Short Woolled, Long Woolled and Mountain. In most breeds there were just two classes, one for wether lambs and one for ewe lambs. The class winners met for the breed championship. Then all the breed champions in each group met to decide the winner of each section. Finally the three remaining pens challenged for the Supreme Championship of the show. This had been won by the Burnham flock of Hampshire Downs in 1930, 1934 and 1935 – a record. The year 1936 saw an innovation from Burnham, two entries in the crossbred Down classes. This came about because the trade for culled ewes the previous year had been so appalling (15s to £1 a head) that it was decided to retain the best ones and run a Southdown ram with them. This proved most successful, but from my point of view it was very special, for I was put in charge of showing the two crossbred pens entered for Smithfield, as Father and the two Wadmans were fully occupied with the Hamps. I was helped by two retired shepherds, both of whom I had known since childhood and who were delighted to have an all-expenses-paid day out at the show. There were twenty-three pens in the ewe lamb class, a great sight and an exacting task for the judge. After what seemed like an eternity, the steward told me to move our pen to the head of the line. Then followed a time that seemed like forever, before I was handed the coveted red rosette. I was over the moon, for Father and Harry had had a look before judging began and had expressed the view that the competition looked so hot that even to get in the awards would be something of a major achievement. If I was over the moon at winning the class, I was at the outer limits of our galaxy when handed the red, white and blue rosette for the breed championship.

My two companions and I were beside ourselves with excitement. Frank, who must have been close on eighty and had been the soul of propriety all the morning, calling me 'Sir', was rather like an old warhorse scenting blood, for he threw his arms around me and, grinning from ear to ear, said, 'Come you on, young feller, we can do it, let's show your dad an' Harry how to show b****y ship [sheep].' The stewards gave us no time to even catch our breath, we were wanted immediately in the main sheep judging ring to compete for the Short Woolled championship. We were the last to arrive, and there, about halfway down the line, were Father and the Wadmans with, for the eighth time, the Hampshire Down breed champions. The looks on their faces were a study, but nothing to what they were going to be!

The judge, having gone carefully over all the exhibits and seen them all move, started discarding and sending out of the ring those he didn't want – it was rather like 'Ten Green Bottles'. At last three pens remained, two from Burnham and a truly magnificent pen of Suffolks. Frank whispered to me, 'We got un, we got un, ours be the best ship.' After much deliberation and making us walk our entries up and down the ring, the judge indicated that he no longer wanted the Hampshires. Father looked positively sick as he left the ring. He had so wanted to set a record by winning the Prince of Wales Gold Cup for the Supreme Championship of the show for the third consecutive year. The judge retired to the far side of the ring, cupped his chin in his hand and looked and looked and looked – I wondered if he was ever going to make up his mind. Father, Harry and Philip stood outside the ring, and I've seldom seen three more anxious faces. At last the judge turned to the steward, took the rosette, walked halfway across the ring and stopped. My heart was in my mouth. Would it never end? Then, smiling, he walked towards us and handed me the rossette. The look of relief on Dad's face was something to behold. He tried to come into the ring with us, but was swiftly told by a steward to remain outside.

There was no let-up. Within minutes, the Mountain and Long Woolled champion pens entered the ring. Frank said, 'We're a' going' to do, I b****y knows it. Keep showin', keep showin'.' I showed as I had never shown before. It is a well-known cliché that half the pedigree goes in through the mouth. Father had another one: 'Showmanship is a third of the conformation when in the ring!'

The judge, a different one, carefully went over the exhibits, then made us walk them up the ring and back. When all three pens had been properly 'stood up' again, he did not hesitate; he took the coveted ribbon, walked across the ring and handed it to me saying, 'Well done, young man. A wonderful pen of lambs. You may never do this again.' He was right. I never did, and I don't think I ever felt more pride in a life of successful showing of almost everything from mice through various breeds of cattle, sheep and pigs than at that moment. Tears were running down Frank's cheeks as, much relieved, Father and the Wadmans joined us in the ring.

When we had returned home and the euphoria had died down, great was the talk and planning for the following year's show. I was preparing a Devon bullock especially for Smithfield and much work had gone into him already, although the show was nearly twelve months ahead. Winners aren't produced overnight. I also had my Dexter steer, Goliath, who was a smasher. Experts who saw him six weeks to a month before the show said they'd never seen his equal, certainly not at Smithfield over the last ten to fifteen years – he had to win the breed championship. My enthusiasm knew no bounds, but I was frustrated by Mother's insisting that I couldn't sleep at the Agricultural Hall the night before judging, with my charges, like herdsmen did, Fred Simpson would be there instead.

At last the day of departure came. A lorry had been booked to take the Devon bullock and Goliath up to London. It was supposed to be at Britwell at 5.30 p.m., but did not turn up until just after 6.00 p.m. Fred had loaded the Devon and I was leading Goliath up the ramp into the lorry when a police constable rode into the yard on his bike. He jumped off and held up his hand.

'Sorry, there's a movement restriction order in force – foot and mouth disease.' I wept. If the lorry had been on time we'd have been safely on the road and out of the area. Sergeant Garrett had gone to the sheep sheds. The exhibits were loaded and Harry Jaycock was actually driving out through the gate as the sergeant arrived and, of course, the sheep were stopped too. The frustration, anger and disappointment were immense. It was a very subdued party that arrived at Islington the next morning as spectators. As Billy Wiltshire and Harry Hobson said to me, as we stood watching and judging, Goliath would have won the breed championship with ease. It didn't make me feel any better!

For two consecutive years we were unable to show at Smithfield due to foot and mouth disease restrictions. In both cases the outbreak was at a livestock dealer's premises within three miles of the estate's boundary. The dealer was not a popular man, but, it was said locally, that the government compensation had made him a rich one. Ironically, foot and mouth disease is not a killer providing proper care is taken, for cattle and other cloven-hoofed animals will quickly get over it. Father, who was a pupil for several years on a remote farm on the edge of Exmoor before the First World War, helped nurse cattle through it. Rubbing salt two or three times a day into the blisters in the mouth and on the tongue and keeping the hooves well packed with stockholm tar will quickly clear it up, and not one beast was lost. Obviously, the outbreak was not reported. That, of course, was strictly illegal.

In the big outbreak in 1920/21, the 2nd Duke of Westminster was allowed, at vast expense, to completely isolate the Home Farms and two whole villages for six months on his Eaton Estate just outside Chester when his Dairy Shorthorn herd was infected by the dreaded disease. Out of five hundred and thirty-one head, only one animal died, not from foot and mouth disease, but from drowning when being drenched late one night! One of the cows which was worst affected, Bare Charm, won the Supreme Dairy Shorthorn Championship at the 1922 Royal Show. But that was all history, long forgotten and it certainly didn't help me with Goliath.

# 11

# *Waste Not, Want Not*

WHILST I was very involved in everything that was going on on the estate, there was always plenty of time to indulge in my many forms of recreation, which when away in the West Country included trout fishing. Every spring Father took a long weekend, combining business with pleasure, and headed off for North Devon. On these visits we often stayed at Beaford with Arthur Leverton and his wife, who lived at Wooley Manor and farmed many lush acres along the banks of the River Torridge. Arthur was a good farmer, but in the 1930s it didn't matter how good you were; it was still a terrible struggle to make a living. So, having a large and beautifully situated home, they started doing bed and breakfast. On hearing that we were off to Wooley Manor, Leslie Wood a great friend of Father's and a brilliant fly fisherman, asked if he could come too. Father happily agreed, but suggested that Leslie should make his own way to the Levertons, for we would be leaving very early as he had several business calls to make at South Molton. These included seeing the auctioneers to whom every year was entrusted the autumn sale of fifteen to twenty Hampshire Down ram lambs from the Burnham flock at their main breeders' sale, and, of course, we couldn't be in South Molton without seeing 'Varmer Sam'.

We reached the manor around 6.00 p.m., to find that Leslie had arrived safely and Mrs Leverton had a meal ready for us. When we'd eaten Arthur suggested a walk down to the river to show Leslie the best places to fish on the morrow and, laughingly, added he might try to sell Dad a wagon of Red Rubies. A walk sounded most inviting, for it was a perfect warm spring evening, the countryside soft and fragrant from the smell of wild flowers and so peaceful – not a man-made sound to be heard. We made our way down towards the river, through the wood, passing great yellow carpets of wild daffodils, so prolific in those days along the Torridge valley.

As we emerged into the first meadow I saw it was very heavily stocked with sheep, as, indeed, was the next one. I looked at Arthur Leverton and raised an eyebrow. He smiled, 'Oh, we're "fixing" the lambs tomorrow.' 'Fixing' was castrating the ram lambs and tailing, or, for the benefit of those who aren't familiar with the term, docking the tails. Father and I went off to look at the Red Rubies, whilst Leslie quietly walked the river bank, watching, almost goggle-eyed, as scores of trout rose to a hatch of fly. The river was full of trout and salmon parr. The trout weren't monsters, far from it, for it was a good fish that made a pound and a half, but they were plump and plentiful, for hardly anyone fished for them, at least not on the water where we were allowed to go. The Torridge was an excellent salmon river and fishing on it was strictly preserved. Thanks to the good offices of my late grandfather, who had been the rector at Beaford, we could fish some five to six miles for trout, which included all the Wooley stretch.

Father, after a little haggling, bought the bullocks and we returned to an excited and enraptured Leslie. It was his first introduction to the delights of North Devon and, like so many before him, he was captivated by the soft beauty of the countryside, the abundance of wildlife and the quiet. As we joined him three pairs of buzzards, once so common in the area, wheeled and soared high overhead, but he wasn't looking at them. He didn't even notice our approach, as his eyes were riveted on the comparatively calm water at the head of a salmon pool. As we joined him, he glanced quickly at us, before pointing. 'Look.' There, just in the shallows, were no fewer than nine salmon. Suddenly, in the centre of the pool, there was a great swirl, followed seconds later by a loud splash, as a fresh-run salmon lept high out of the water, gleaming silver in the evening sunlight, before falling back into the river. Leslie was beside himself with excitement.

'What would happen if I hooked a salmon on a trout fly? Such things do happen.' Arthur laughed.

'Well, in the unlikely event of your landing it, I'd have to take it up to the General, who owns the fishing rights on this stretch of the river and ... I suppose, if a water bailiff came along, you'd be summoned for taking salmon without a licence.' Leslie's face fell, but not for many minutes, for, as we sauntered quietly along the bank Arthur suddenly stopped and, putting a finger to his lips, pointed.

There, about thirty yards upstream, an otter was emerging from the river onto the shingle beach below the bank. It was carrying something that flailed around its head like a whiplash and looked like an eel. We all froze and watched. It was obvious that the otter had not seen us, for it settled down to feed. Suddenly, Arthur sneezed. The otter's head jerked up, saw us and disappeared like a wraith into the fast-flowing river. When we reached the spot where it had been, I clambered down the bank. I could hardly believe my eyes, for there lay not the remains of an eel, but of a grass snake. I tossed it up onto the field for the others to see. I had, on several occasions, when fishing, seen a grass snake swim the river and it always fascinated me how they seemed to oscillate across the surface, but I certainly had never thought of them as being the possible prey of otters.

Next morning I was awake by 6.00 a.m. a bit too late for the dawn chorus, but still the sound of bird song echoed all around the manor. As I lay listening, counting how many different ones I could identify, I heard one of the Levertons go downstairs. I jumped out of bed, slipped on a dressing gown and went to the kitchen. Arthur was standing by the big wood-burning range, waiting for a kettle to boil. All the heating in the manor was by wood. There was masses of it on the farm, so why buy coal at 3s 6d a hundredweight? Arthur smiled and greeted me warmly.

'You're up early. Didn't you sleep well?'

'Like a log. I'm usually up around this time. What are you going to do?'

'Have a cup of tea, then help the lads bring the sheep up to the pens.'

'Can I come?'

'Of course.' I raced off upstairs and hurriedly dressed. As we set out through the back entrance to the farmyard, we passed Mary, the live-in maid. I'd known her since I was a child, for she was a niece of old man Bright, who had been my grandfather's gardener at the rectory for years. She was busily picking the young shoots of stinging nettles and putting them into a large wicker basket, and she wasn't wearing gloves. I called 'Good morning' to her and then added, 'Gosh, that must hurt.' She just smiled, waved and continued with her harvest.

We were back for breakfast by 8.30 a.m. Father had been up some while and had put up our rods, tied on our favourite flies and was ready for the off as soon as we'd had breakfast. This was a real farmhouse one: two eggs, several rashers of good fat home-cured bacon, homemade sausages, fried potato and fried bread. Leslie, who had just appeared, rubbed his hands together and set to work with a vengeance – declaring he was famished. Mrs Leverton came into the dining room, just as we had finished, to see if anyone would like more. We all laughed and said we'd had enough to last us all day.

'I hope not. I'm preparing a special lunch, one we normally have only once a year. Do you think you could be back by one o'clock?' We assured her that we could. Before we left for the river I went through to the kitchen to collect an apple for each of us, just in case we felt peckish during the morning. Mary was busy at the sink stripping the leaves off the stalks of a great pile of nettles. I noticed her hands looked red and swollen, but she didn't seem to be worrying.

As we made our way down through the wood, close to the sheep pens, where several of the farmhands were busy separating the ewes out from the lambs, the shepherd waved to us and wished us luck. Soon all three of us were wading the river, casting energetically. We had agreed we'd take nothing under nine inches which would mean any fish we kept would be around three quarters of a pound. It was a glorious morning, enough sun to make it pleasant, but not too much to spoil the fishing. It was warm, bringing about an almost continuous hatch of fly. There was a gentle westerly wind and it was almost a case of a trout of some size every cast, thus proving the truth of the old adage, my grandfather had taught me when I first started fishing: 'When the wind is in the west, then the fishes bite the best.'

We were a happy and contented trio that started back for lunch. We propped our rods up just inside the wood as there was no fear that anyone would touch them, and continued on to the house, jacking off our waders in the porch. Arthur greeted us in the hall.

'When you're ready, I've a nice little refresher for you in the dining room.' When we had foregathered Arthur produced a great flagon of home-made cider. He filled two pint glasses and handed them to Father and Leslie. As he poured one for himself he asked, 'What about Michael?' Dad laughed, 'Why not? He can have a small one. If it has any effect on him, it'll only go to his legs and not his head. I know this home-brewed cider and what it can do from bitter experience years ago on Exmoor – it can be lethal on the legs.' We sat chatting and supping our drinks.

Leslie was really enjoying himself: he'd caught nine keepable fish and a whopper of one and three-quarter pounds. The door opened and Mrs Leverton entered with a huge dish, piled high with what she announced were sweetbreads in batter. She was followed closely by Mary bearing a tray with an equally large dish of spinach and a hot crispy home-made loaf. The Levertons joined us and, on his own admission, Leslie made a pig of himself, for he had three helpings of sweetbreads. He said he had seldom tasted anything so delicious and certainly the spinach, done with cream, was the best he'd ever had. The main course was followed by apple tart and Devonshire cream – a cup of tea and we were away again to the river.

As we passed close to the sheep pens, all was activity. Leslie wanted to take a closer look. One gang were tailing, whilst the shepherd and a helper were castrating the ram lambs, tossing the testes into a bucket as he nicked them out. The day of castration with rubber rings was still to come. The shepherd grinned and asked if we'd enjoyed our dinner. Leslie replied that he had and they were quite the best sweetbreads he'd ever tasted. The shepherd laughed and said he was looking forward to his tea, as he, too, would be having sweetbreads. As we walked away Leslie looked thoughtful. Suddenly he stopped and turned to Father. 'Where do all these sweetbreads come from? I mean they're quite scarce any time I try to get some from our butcher.'

Father winked at me. 'Where do you think? Out of the bucket you've just been looking at, of course.'

Leslie blanched. 'You don't mean that what we had for lunch were lamb's . . .?'

'Yes, I do, and the spinach was young nettles. We'll probably have nice crisply roasted, or fried lambs' tails for supper.'

Leslie turned even paler and developed a greenish hue before making a sudden rush to a nearby bush, behind which he lost his lunch. When he returned father stood laughing at him.

'That was silly. You were perfectly happy when you thought it was the thymus gland, for that's what sweetbreads are, and you eat liver and kidneys, which are basically filters, so what's so terrible with what you had? Nothing like as revolting as those snails you say you're so fond of.' Leslie didn't answer, just picked up his rod and headed off to the river. By tea time he'd come to, saying he'd been silly to react as he did to learning what the 'sweetbreads' really were; it was just the sudden thought. He admitted they were excellent and he'd never have believed that nettles could be so succulent. After several glasses of the home-brew, he thoroughly enjoyed his supper of crispy fried lambs' tails, followed by Torridge trout, topped off with Mrs Leverton's excellent homemade cheese – Wooley Manor was very self-sufficient!

At Burnham the 'fixing' time for the lambs always produced plenty of takers for the 'by-products' and we annually had lambs' tails, but Mother wouldn't, much to Father's annoyance, have anything to do with 'sweetbreads'. Another thing considered a delicacy by many of the old-timers was young rooks. The rookeries were shot every year in the spring; it was something that had to be done, like keeping down the rabbit population. Rooks can do a lot of good in feeding off leatherjackets and wireworm, but, equally, they do tremendous damage pulling up sprouted grain in search of these and, if other food is in short supply, will really set to work on freshly sown corn. When the two rookeries were shot, Father would gather up the bag, leaving some at Britwell and some at Lynch Hill for the staff to help themselves, and there were never any left. Again, Mother wouldn't 'play'. She said she couldn't stand the smell and I must admit I agreed with her. There is an art in making a rook pie so that the smell does not permeate the finished article, and those who have the knack can produce a most appetising dish. As rooks were off the ration during the war, there was a ready market in them, particularly to some of the top London restaurants, where they were served up as game pie.

In the 1930s pig trade was so bad that Father decided to kill one, sometimes two, porkers a week on the estate, to sell to the staff, something which was much appreciated. The actual butchering was no problem, for Jim Light, before he became a cowman, had served his apprenticeship in the trade. The price was based on one penny a pound more than what the pigs would have made in Slough Market. This meant the choice cuts were 4d or 5d per pound, undercutting the butchers and saving employees money. Nothing was wasted, as everything was sold, right down to the trotters.

Such perks as I have outlined were much appreciated by all the estate workers, but one employee remained aloof and uninterested – old Murkett (I never knew his Christian name), who looked after the small herd of Jersey cows at the Home Farm. In the farmyard, as was common in those days, were a couple of pigsties, where weaners would be sent to fatten, their ration being supplemented every day with buckets of swill from the house. During the late 1920s and early 1930s the cook-cum-housekeeper would discard any food that had been into the dining room as being unsuitable for use in the servants' hall and would relegate nearly whole joints, chickens, pies and various other dishes to the swill bucket. Murkett had quickly cottoned on to this and supplied two additional buckets of his own, one for meat and one for puddings. For the small consideration of sixpence per week, he persuaded the scullerymaid, who was responsible for putting out the swill, to assign all the unspoilt edible 'swill' to his personal buckets. It would not be an exaggeration to say he lived off the fat of the land at virtually no expense. As he once said to Tom Rose and me, 'I be the only b****r as eats as well as the guvnor.'

Sadly, for him, the days of manna were to come to an abrupt end. E. C. B. had a habit of getting Father to call, on a Monday morning, to discuss various matters whilst he was having his breakfast, before leaving for the City. One morning when Father went through to the breakfast room, he was greeted petulantly with, 'I've hundreds and hundreds of hens at Lees Farm. How is it I never have a brown egg for my breakfast? I like brown eggs.'

Father laughed and replied, 'Well, it appears cook requires thirty dozen eggs a week and that is what is delivered, in two lots, Mondays and Fridays throughout the year, and there should be plenty of brown eggs amongst them.'

E. C. B. was furious and, at the earliest opportunity, instigated a full investigation. Cook had, for many years, had a nice little sideline supplying her contacts in the village with eggs, butter, cream and other produce. It goes without saying that her departure was immediate. From then on only twelve dozen eggs were required weekly at The Grove – all brown! And the new cook had more sensible ideas about dealing with leftovers.

## 12

# *Perambulations and Percherons*

BEFORE the Second World War there was a far greater inclination, indeed necessity, for people to walk than there is today. Children thought nothing of walking several miles to school, whatever the weather; whilst many of the older farmhands trudged two to three miles, or more, to reach their place of work by 7 a.m. Others, of course, were mobile, in so far as they had bicycles. I can just remember, in the early 1920s, one old boy (he must have been heading up towards seventy) who regularly rode into Britwell farmyard and, of course, out in the evening, on a penny farthing, a product of the previous century and the forerunner of the bicycle. It had one huge wheel, a small one at the back and required considerable skill to mount it, never mind ride it. He was asked why he didn't buy a modern bike, to which he had replied that his penny farthing had done him well for the past forty years and he saw no reason to waste £5 on one of them new-fangled things or thirty bob to £2 on a secondhand one.

It was commonplace for a man, having walked to work, to take a team of horses and follow them all day at plough, or, in the spring, a single horse and spend the day 'horse-hoeing' root crops, plodding steadily up and down the rows cutting out the weeds. In either case, the horseman would cover a good eight to nine miles a day and then at 5.00 p.m., unless called on to do overtime, start the long trudge home.

Following a pair of horses all day was nothing like as arduous as some jobs. Over the years, keeping to Father's dictum that I should have practical experience in every job I might eventually oversee in the years to come, I tried them all. Without any doubt my *bête noire* was pulling mangolds – a real killer.

In pre-war days mangolds were universally grown on any farm wintering livestock. Provided they did not get frosted they would keep until the spring. Cattle loved them, for they were sweet, but analysis proved that their nutritive value was negligible and they were very labour intensive. This combination led to their demise. and one would have to travel a long, long way to find a field of mangolds these days. In fact I suspect it would be nearly impossible.

I had a go at mangold pulling only a couple of times, and that was enough. We worked in pairs, usually taking four rows each, moving from the centre outwards. You pulled a mangold (some were very weighty) and, gripping the leaves, swung it towards the heap into which it was to go, at the same time cutting through the stem with a 'trimmer', so that the mangold landed on the heap and you were left holding the greenery. It was a back-breaking and tiring job. Bend, pull, swing, cut, bend, pull, swing, cut – it never seemed to end. The 'trimmers' were made up by 'Old Jay' from discarded scythe blades, were fitted with handles by Charles Davis and were kept razor sharp.

The heaps in the field were half the size of a dung cart's capacity. If there was any likelihood of frost in the night, the tops were scraped up with four grained dung-forks and spread over the heaps. Once pulled, carting would start. This entailed throwing up the mangolds, by hand, into the carts. More backbreaking and tiring work. When the land was soft, a trace-horse was often needed to help the one between the shafts pull the load out on to a farm lane or a main road.

Clamps were constructed as close as possible to the place where the mangolds would be used. These were about eight feet across the base, building up to a ridge about five feet high. There was quite an art in stacking and building a straight and symmetrical clamp, and the whole would be covered with a foot or more of straw and a trench dug around it, the soil being thrown up to form a crust, keeping the straw in place, as well as making it even more frost proof. 'Chimnies' of straw were left every four or five feet, so that the clamp could 'breathe'. Sometimes clamps were stored in a building, but still well insulated with straw.

When the time came to start using the mangolds, the clamp would be opened and a man would lift each one to trim off the roots and scrape off the mud. The 'trimmer' for this purpose was slightly different from those used when harvesting the crop. It had a hook at the end of the spine to which the blade was attached and one lifted the mangolds with this – a great saving on the back! When enough were cleaned they would be barrowed to a rootcutter. Latterly these could be power driven, usually by a small petrol engine, but the first ones I remember were hand operated. The cutter sliced the mangolds, or any other roots, into fingers about four to five inches long and an inch thick, and these were spread out on the floor. Then meal, such as ground barley and crushed oats, was added, before being well mixed and fed to stock.

When pulping and feeding any root crop to cattle, it was always advisable to have a probang handy. This was a long, very flexible rod with a knob on the end. Often larger pieces would fall through the bottom of the rootcutter and it was not unusual for one of these to get stuck in a beast's throat, or halfway down the oesophagus. When this happened, the animal would choke to death if the obstruction was not quickly removed. If the animal's head was held high, and the probang was passed over the back of the tongue, the blockage could be pushed down into the stomach – rather like rodding a drain!

Shanks's pony was a favoured way of moving livestock over shortish distances, of anything up to five miles, and it was a common sight to see cattle and sheep being driven into the local market, in our case Slough, adjacent to the railway station and in the centre of the town, or to pastures new along the public highway. Livestock took precedence over motor vehicles and it was as common then to be delayed by herds of dairy cows, sedately making their way back to the farmyard for milking, as it is today by endless miles of cones on motorways.

The enjoyment of the countryside was added to every spring by the government-sponsored Hunter Improvement Society's travelling stallions. They were a welcome sight, for horses were part of everyday life, of the agricultural economy and, indeed, the army. When war broke out in 1939, hundreds of horses were commandeered for active service. One had no option, for commandeer meant exactly that and, eventually, the owner received a niggardly payment for what, in many cases, was a much-loved pet, and many of these had been sired by H.I.S. stallions.

The stallions had regular routes, stopping overnight at the same place each week. Solan, a lovely 16.2 hands bay, used to put up every Wednesday night at Lees Farm. He was kept immaculate by the stallion-man Ted, a very dapper person who, it was rumoured, was as much sought after as his charge! All the grooms carried their clothes and other belongings in a waterproof roll, attached to a surcingle, across the stallion's back. From this two side-reins led to the bit; these and the bridle were polished to a high degree, as was the leather lead rein, with its shining brass chain at the end, which was attached to the bit. Being a stallion-man was no job for a slouch, for each day the stallion would cover twelve to fifteen miles, calling at various prearranged places to attend to any mares that might require his service. The stud fee for a halfbred mare was two guineas and for a thoroughbred, five. Both horse and man had to be and indeed were, fit, for they travelled the circuit for about three months.

One year, in the mid-1930s, something happened to Solan and he had to be withdrawn He was replaced, at short notice, by a stallion sent down from Scotland – Raperie. He was black, not the most amiable horse I ever met, but certainly the most erotic. I was at Lees Farm, deputising for Father, when he arrived. His groom, Jock, was a very dour Scot. I never saw him smile once during the weeks he visited the farm, but, worse still, he had such a pronounced Scottish accent that it was very hard to understand much of what he said. The first, somewhat anxious, question he asked me had to be repeated several times before I could understand: 'Are there any stinging nettles around?' I replied that there were and that there was a big patch at the back of one of the barns. He asked if he could see them. Surprised, but ever ready to oblige, I took Jock off to view the nettles. To my amazement he strode out into the near waist high patch, pulled up the sleeve of his jacket and plunged his arm into them, quickly withdrawing it with a curse. 'Aye, aye, them'll do.' I would have been less than human if I hadn't asked what they would do for. With difficulty I learned that Raperie would not cover a mare unless he'd had a good roll in nettles. It was Jock's first time south of the border and, it seemed, he considered us all to be so nambypamby that he thought our nettles might not have the 'bite' of Scottish ones. Later I told Cyril Barker, the head poultryman at the Lees, about the incident. He burst out laughing and said that had Jock been wearing a kilt, he'd have had his doubts more quickly disproved.

This erogenous stallion I had to see in action. Having made sure Jock had all he needed, I rode off on my bike to Billy Oliver's stables only a few hundred yards away and regaled Dolly Harding, the girl in charge of the yard, and her helpers with the latest news from Lees Farm. There were two mares of Billy's to be tried, one at about half past five and another at around 7.30 p.m. It looked as though Raperie was in for a busy evening. I fervently hoped we wouldn't run out of nettles! Later I returned to the farm. Jock had had his tea, which I gathered was to his satisfaction. In silence we waited for the first of Billy Oliver's mares. It had to be in silence for, it seemed, my accent was as big an obstacle to Jock as his was to me. We tried the mare; she was ready. Jock led Raperie off to the bed of nettles, and within seconds he was rolling happily and obviously enjoying the experience. After two or three minutes he got to his feet, shook himself and curled back his top lip – it was the nearest I'd seen to a smile since the Scottish invasion. Eleven months later the mare, Daggles, whom Billy had bought as a riding school hack off a gypsy, produced a bonnie foal; not entirely surprisingly the girls at the stables christened it Nettles.

As well as the H.I.S. stallions, it was not unusual to pass a Shire stallion travelling in a similar fashion, but by the latter part of the 1930s this was becoming something of a rarity, at least in the south of the county. However, I remember several times, north of Aylesbury, meeting a magnificent Shire that was dark brown, almost black, and must have been all of 18 hands high. His mane and tail were carefully braided, with plumes all along the crest of his neck – a real picture of power and beauty.

I came to know Stanley Chivers very well. He managed the farms owned by Chivers jams just outside Cambridge. Once I had the pleasure of staying with him for two days and being shown around the farms, totalling just over 10,000 acres. It was a wonderful experience, but, undoubtedly, the highlight of my visit was when Stanley took me to see eight teams of magnificent grey Percherons at plough in a field of stubble. All the horses had their manes and tails plaited up with red and green ribbons, whilst the ploughmen were dressed alike in brown overall coats, fawn breeches, brown boots and leggings and matching caps – it was a most majestic sight, one which certainly enriched the countryside and, sadly, one which will never be seen again. Chivers Farms had by far the largest stud of Percherons, in the country. The breed originated from the Perche district in northern France and with their comparatively dean legs (that is, lack of hair around the fetlocks) in comparison with Shires, it was not difficult to visualise them as quick, active chargers at the battle of Agincourt.

Apart from work, far more people walked for pleasure in the 1920s and 1930s than do today. It was a common sight along any country road to see both mothers and nannies pushing prams, elderly people taking their daily constitutional and youngsters out for a stroll, enjoying the countryside and the sounds of nature. They didn't need a Walkman blaring in their ears! I found that a walk around the estate was never without interest, but some became memorable, such as on a warm evening in early June, when I visited the old disused gravel pits beyond Lynch Hill Farm, on land rented off Slough Trading Estate. Several weeks before, I had been thrilled to spot a pair of red-backed shrikes and, even better, found their nest. They seemed very shy and disappeared when their territory was invaded. Because of this I kept well away, except for one quick inspection of the nest – the hen had laid six eggs. These lovely birds are frequently known as butcher-birds, because of their strange habit of making 'larders' by impaling their prey on thorns and leaving them until needed. They are almost hawk like in the way that they hunt, in so far as they select a high vantage point, where they perch, motionless, until they spot some delicacy, when they swoop down, grab their quarry and quickly add it to their larder.

In addition to the alternative name of butcher-bird, the red-backed shrike has a variety of local names throughout the country, such as 'Murdering pie', 'Nine-killer' and 'Whiskey John'. I can easily follow the reasoning behind the first two, but can't, for the life of me, think of an explanation for the latter.

On the evening in question I took up my position on the far side of the gravel pit from the shrikes' nest, settled myself comfortably and took out my binoculars from their case. There was great activity around the nest and it was obvious that the eggs had hatched. I must have watched them for nearly two hours. I spotted where the 'larder' was situated (I hadn't found it at the time of my visit), undoubtedly in a blackthorn some five or six yards from the nest. I noted, with interest, that the hen constantly took what she caught straight to her brood, whilst the cock seemed to rotate between the nest and the larder.

At last I decided I must go, but before I did I intended taking a quick look at both the nest and the larder. I scrambled down the side of the pit, made my way across it and climbed up the other side. A few strides and I had reached my objective and peered in. There were five nestlings, which, I guessed, were about four days old. I didn't delay, for the parent birds were becoming very agitated. I moved over to the blackthorn. The larder was well stocked with a variety of goodies – at least as far as shrikes are concerned. Impaled on thorns were a number of large moths of different varieties, caterpillars, small frogs, several species of beetles, even a half-grown mouse – quite a selection!

Reluctantly I left and made my way back along the edge of the pit. As I did so I saw Bob Hedges walking up the cart-track from the direction of Hay Mill pond, and when I reached the point where our paths would cross, I waited for him. Bob had been going round his partridge nests. Most of them had hatched and the broods gone, but a few late ones were still left. It was the custom, on any well-keepered shoot, for the gamekeepers to pick up the eggs, daily, as they were laid, replacing them with dummy ones. When the hen had finished laying, these were replaced by the real thing and the nests carefully monitored. Bob kept a record of all the nests he found (probably about 90 per cent of those on his beat), the number of eggs laid, the date they hatched and the number of clear or infertile eggs. As I walked along with him I told him of my 'shrike watch'. Apparently, when he was a beat keeper on a big estate in Wiltshire, two pairs nested, for several seasons, within the area he cared for, much of which bordered on the downs. On numerous occasions he had found the common brown lizard, at one time regularly to be seen in dry areas throughout the country, in the shrikes's larders – some quite small, others adults of four to five inches. The latter says much for the tenacity of these lovely birds, for their overall length is not more than six to seven inches.

Another evening stroll which is indelibly impressed on my memory was in the summer of 1938. It was towards the end of my first year at Reading University. It, too, was in June, warm, sunny – the sort of evening I had to be out of doors. We were in the middle of end of year exams, but I really felt I needed a break from revision. So, taking a gun out of the case and calling Sally, Father's bull terrier, I set off down the lane. Apart from clearing my head and getting some fresh air, I wanted three rabbits for the ferrets and our two ravens, Oswald and Twisle, the latter being a fairly recent addition to our menagerie. They had been orphaned, rescued and reared in captivity. However, when fully grown no attempt had been made to return them to the wild and, when they came to us, they were eleven years old and completely domesticated. I reached the end of the lane, Sally happily trotting by my side, crossed the main road, brushed through the hedge into Nobb's Crook and set out diagonally across the field for the far end of Lammas Wood. The previous year it had been planted with barley, undersown with Montgomery red clover. There had been a massive crop, all now safely ricked awaiting the arrival of Jim Stannett, the thatcher, who travelled far and wide to his work in a pony and trap.

The clover was already starting to sprout again, providing succulent shoots for the ever-present, ever-hungry rabbits. With Sally hunting the ground ahead of me, I quickly shot what I needed, much to Sally's delight, for not only was she a good hunter, but an excellent retriever as well. I continued to the end of the wood, then turned back through this, heading for Lynch Hill lane. I was nearly at the stile leading into the grass field that adjoined the lane when something, literally, whistled past my ear, followed by a thud just behind me to the left. Fractionally later I heard a crack – the sound of a .22 rifle being fired. I ran forward and there in the lane was a man with a gun, obviously a rifle. I dropped my shotgun and the rabbits, jumped over the stile and started to sprint across the hundred and fifty yards or so to the lane. However, the man saw me, leaped onto his bike and pedalled off up the hill.

It was no good trying to pursue him, so I returned to the wood to collect my gun and rabbits. Just as I reached the stile Bob Hedges appeared, coming along the ride from the opposite direction. I told him what had happened. He laughed and said I must have imagined that something had whistled past my ear, for if the man with the rifle had been taking a pot shot at a rabbit and missed, the bullet was more likely to have passed my ankle than my ear. This seemed logical, but I was sure I hadn't been mistaken and started to examine the the tree.

Within seconds I found a fresh hole in the bark. Bob and I set to work to dig with our pocket knives. After several minutes I struck something hard. Further excavation uncovered a steel-nosed .22 bullet embedded a good two to three inches into the tree, which, incidentally, was oak. Bob made me stand by the hole and he estimated that had I been two and a half feet to the left, it would have caught me squarely in the middle of the forehead. Not a happy thought, but as Sergeant Carrett, to whom I reported the incident, said later, 'A miss is as good as a mile.'

The police never found out who the man was, although they checked all the people in the locality who had firearm certificates and their whereabouts at the time the shot was fired. The chances were that the bullet came from an unlicensed rifle. I carried it as a sort of lucky charm up to and through the war years, but finally lost it though a hole in my pocket. As a friend said, it was better to have lost it like that than have kept it through a hole in the head.

# 13

# University Years

ON looking back it seems nothing short of miraculous that I went to university when I think of the salary Father was earning – £650 per annum. There were no student grants, and although a few bursaries were available, I didn't qualify. Like my brother, Ralph, before me and a very limited number of other students, I was granted the special dispensation of being allowed to live at home and motor to Reading every day. First-year students were not normally allowed to have a car, however wealthy they might be, and such rules were rigorously enforced. Some, braver than others, flouted this and kept a car secretly in town.

I travelled to Reading in a super little Austin 10 saloon, APH 694. It was three years old when Father bought it from William Sands, who owned and ran the garage in Burnham High Street. The estate did a lot of business with him and so I am sure Father received a most favourable deal. The car was a 1934 model, had just under 40,000 miles on the clock and the asking price was £70. Father bid £60 and a deal was quickly struck at £65. I was allowed six gallons of petrol a week, which cost about 10½d per gallon and I could charge to Father's account; anything over this amount I had to pay for myself.

I also received an allowance of 10s (50p) per week to cover lunch in the university buttery and cups of coffee with fellow students between lectures, either in the buttery or at various cafés around the town. A particular favourite was Sally's, very chintzy, with charming and cheery waitresses, all I'm sure designed to attract the students, but it was pricey – 3d for a cup of coffee! If one was really pushing the boat out and had a fancy cake, it cost 6d – it was a pretty special girl that received that sort of treatment. Usually we went dutch. My allowance also paid for my cigarettes, beer and visits to the cinema.

We all lived life to the full, but it was seldom I overspent and had to draw on my reserves – carefully saved money I had collected over the years from the bounty on rats and various other vermin and, of course, from the sale of surplus purebred rabbits, pigeons and bantams.

Depending on the time of year, if I ran short of ready cash it didn't necessarily mean delving into my savings. In winter I just took my garden-gun, fitted with a spotlight, and went off around the rickyards shooting rats. Carrying a bounty of 2d a tail, six would more than pay for an extra gallon of petrol, a round of drinks with my friends, or allow me to take *the* girl of the moment to Sally's for a coffee and a fancy cake or sticky bun. Once I persuaded a real smasher from the Art Department to go to Sally's with me. As I went to pay, she, as was customary, offered her share. Laughingly I said, 'No, no, this is on me. I had a great evening at the rats last night.' She looked bewildered and asked me to explain. I told her about the bounty. She positively gagged, claimed I'd been entertaining her with 'blood money' and swept out – end of romance!

Life was good, for I had the best of both worlds. If I had lectures only in the morning or in the afternoon, then the other half of the day I could spend at home, pursuing my many and varied interests, when not studying. Quite often I would get detailed, by Father, to some job on one of the farms, usually with livestock. This I enjoyed, but must admit that at times, I felt somewhat piqued at his policy of no pay, except for jobs being taken on a piecework by the staff, when I, too, could take a hoe or whatever, and get the same rates as they did.

Once a week the students went out to the university farm at Sonning for a 'practical walk'. My popularity on these occasions was beyond the capacity of APH, but I usually had four passengers. I was, to say the least, a bit blasé over these excursions and, at times, highly amused. Our tours were conducted by Mr Black, a lecturer on the arable side of farming and, as it happened, my tutor. He, also, had much to say in the planning and management of the farm. It was he who introduced a number of Aylesbury ducks on a free-range basis, with wooden arks for shelter – I suppose a couple of hundred in all. We, of course, were given details as to what they cost, the ration they were receiving and the estimated sale price when fattened. I and another student, who like me had grown up on a large farm, worked out the viability of the ducks and, when taking into account depreciation on the arks, came to the conclusion that, at the best, they might just break even, but more probably make a loss.

The next time we were at Sonning, my friend and I put our figures to Mr Black. He didn't seemed impressed by our industriousness and questioned the accuracy of our findings. Then he, obviously, had an inspiration, for he said, 'Ah yes, but you have missed something most important – the consolidating effect of their feet on the soil. Consolidation is an all-important factor in producing a good crop, be it corn or grass.' There was complete silence, for we were, to use a modern expression, truly gobsmacked. Then we started to laugh as the absurdity of Mr Black's statement sank in, for the average weight of the ducks at the time could not have been more than about three pounds. That evening when I got home and told Father, to begin with he thought it hilarious; then he changed his mind and said he wondered why he was spending good money to send me to a university to listen to such claptrap.

In fairness, I must say that Mr Black's *faux pas* was not in keeping with the general high standard of tuition, although those of us with practical experience found the predictions of one junior lecturer somewhat improbable and, indeed, highly amusing. He seriously assured us that a time would come when farmyard manure would be outdated and the fertility in the soil would come out of a bag. About once a term we had a tête à tête with the head of the faculty, Professor Rae. I put this prognosis to him. He smiled benignly and said, 'My dear Twist, wherever did you get such an extraordinary idea?' In view of his reaction I thought it best not to say from one of his staff and hastily replied that I'd been studying a paper on work recently done at the Oxford University Farm on this subject, which was true. I was commended for my diligence, but the professor assured me I could put such wild ideas from my mind.

It was about a week before Christmas and a few days into our end of term break when I was driving back one evening from The Crown at East Burnham, where I'd been enjoying a half of bitter and a game of darts, partnered by Bob Hedges. Actually, I'd enjoyed three halves, for Bob and I had won both our games and it was always a case of 'loser buys'. I had bought Bob a drink when I'd arrived, as well as one for myself, and my evening had cost only 6d. I was in fact feeling very flush, for Father had said he would continue my allowance throughout the holiday period. I took the road home that ran to the north-west of the estate, bordering Burnham golf course, leaving Cants Hill and the main woods away to my left. There was a reasonably wide grass verge to this and as I drove along the headlights showed up a number of horses tethered along it and beyond them a caravan. As I passed I saw there was a cheerful fire and sitting by it were my friends Johnny and Tilly. I pulled up and walked back. I received a warm welcome and Tilly offered me a cup of cocoa. I declined, but seated myself on the caravan steps to have a gossip – I hadn't seen them since mid summer. Tilly seemed in excellent spirits, but Johnny seemed a bit uptight.

'Something's worrying you, isn't it Johnny?'

'Yes. That so-and-so Bill Yeoman was along here, on his motor bike, about an hour ago. He had the b****y cheek to tell me to move on and I told him, quick, what I did on the public highway had nothing to do with him and to clear off.' Johnny gave a dry laugh, 'He did, too, when I started to walk towards him. He's a gutless b****r if ever I saw one, but I'll have the last laugh come tomorrow morning.'

'What are you going to do?'

'Why, get our Christmas dinner of course.' He sat quietly for at least a minute, then said, 'You've always been wanting to know what I keep my gamecocks for.

Well, if you're here around 6.30 tomorrow morning, I'll show you. That is if you promise not to dob on me.'

'Before I promise anything, what are you going to do?'

Johnny was again silent, then laughed. 'Well, either of my two boys, I call them David and Goliath, will kill a cock pheasant in seconds. I wait before dawn by a feedride and when an old cock flies down from his roost I let one, of the boys go. You know how cock pheasants spar. Well, as soon as the pheasant sees my rooster, he'll try and see him off and that's where he makes a big mistake. He'd be no match anyway, but I fix steel fighting spurs on my lads and it's all over in seconds. Do you want to see them in action?'

'I must admit I'd love to, Johnny, but I can't condone you poaching Mr Clifton-Brown's pheasants. I wish you hadn't told me. Supposing I was to go with you and we were caught? It'd look good, wouldn't it, the agent's son nicked, in the company of a gypsy, illegally taking game?' Johnny gave a deep laugh.

'No fear of that, I haven't been caught for years. My three girls [his lurchers] stand guard at various vantage points and will be back to warn me at the slightest hint of trouble. Then either I scarper or lie low 'till the danger's past and, if the impossible happened and that blundering elephant, Bill Yeoman, should stumble across us, I'd say you'd just caught me.'

'That's all very well, but it'd still be poaching.'

'So what?' The guvnor's not going to miss a couple of cock pheasants out of all he's got. I'll bet he'll have a good Christmas dinner, so why shouldn't Tilly and I?'

I stood up. 'I'll see.' As I drove home my mind was in a turmoil. I knew what I should do – tell Father, but, if I did and a trap was set, the chances were that Johnny's girls would warn him before he walked into it and I'd be made to look a right fool. I slept badly that night and was wide awake by five. To go or not to go?

That was the question and I didn't know the answer. I lay in bed trying to make up my mind. Eventually, youthful curiosity got the better of me.

I slipped out of bed, quickly dressed, went downstairs and took my bike out of the garage. Minutes later I was speeding past Britwell Farm along the road that led to Burnham Grove and on to Cants Hill. I still wasn't sure whether I was going to try to stop Johnny or do what I really wanted to and go with him. I left my bike in the field and approached the caravan, and I was just able to see the three lurchers appear like shadows from underneath it. They didn't make a sound. I was wondering what to do, when, suddenly, a voice said, 'You've come then.' I nearly died – I hadn't heard Johnny come up behind me.

When I had got over the shock, I said, 'Yes, well, I thought I ought to try and stop you.'

Johnny gave a chuckle. 'Not a hope, unless you tell on me. I'm not going to clear the covert, which I could do, only take a couple of birds for our Christmas dinner. You may as well come. I meant what I said last night; I won't let you get into any trouble.' After a moment's hesitation, I agreed.

'Fine. Now, once we leave the road, no talking.' just then I heard a muffled cackle and looked down. Johnny was holding what appeared to be a box; it was too dark to really see. He must have sensed where I was looking and quietly said, 'That's Goliath. I'm only taking one this morning. As soon as dawn breaks, I don't reckon we'll be more than ten or fifteen minutes. I had a thorough scout around when the moon came up soon after midnight and know exactly where we're going. If I'd wanted to, I could have filled a sack by using a snare on the end of a pole. Pheasants are terribly stupid birds. Come on, let's go.'

We went back along the road to the gate into the field where I'd left my bike. We entered quietly, then instead of going straight across the field, as I would have done, Johnny turned right-handed and followed round in the shadow of the hedge until we came to the wood. I knew that a few yards to our left was a stile over the rabbit fence leading onto a feed-ride. Then we reached it Johnny clicked his fingers. His three girls cleared it immediately and I could just make out their silhouette as they stood waiting. Johnny signalled me to go next. Once we were all in the wood, by some sign from their owner that I did not see, the girls glided off silently in different directions to take up their positions. We made our way down the ride to Johnny's chosen spot behind a small clump of snowberry. Johnny took the gamecock out of the box, and it happily settled down in the crook of his arm.

Two owls called to each other; otherwise there was an uncanny quiet throughout the wood. We waited in silence for about ten minutes before dawn was heralded by a few, almost flute-like, calls of a blackbird, quickly joined by one or two hesitant, rich full notes of a songthrush. Within minutes, as the sky lightened in the east, the wood became alive. Suddenly, with a clatter of wings, a cock pheasant landed on the ride not ten yards away. Johnny bent down and quietly pushed Goliath forward. The gamecock strutted out to the centre of the ride, flapped his wings and crowed. The pheasant immediately responded, advancing aggressively, feathers ruffled. My view was largely impaired by the bush, so all I saw was a flurry of feathers, followed by a triumphant crow from Goliath. Johnny, silent as a mouse, slipped out onto the ride, scooped up his 'gladiator', plus the pheasant and, was back before I hardly had time to realise he'd gone.

It was light enough to see that there were a number of pheasants out feeding, but no cocks close to us. Then one came winging down the ride, to land right in front of us. Johnny again pushed Goliath forward. He swaggered out, head high and threw out his challenge. There was rather more preliminary sparring than the first time before the gamecock went in for the kill, but it was no contest, Goliath being armed with steel spurs. Johnny gathered up victor and victim, which he put in a sack with the first half of his Christmas dinner.

He stood stroking the colourful plumage of his conqueror as he quietly talked to him in a crooning voice. As I watched it was obvious that Johnny was filling his mouth with saliva. Then, much to my surprise, he held the cock up to his lips and the latter quite clearly drank from them. When he seemed to have had his fill, Johnny put him back in his box and gently closed the lid. As he stood up, I asked Johnny why he'd let Goliath do what he had. It didn't seem very hygienic to me. Johnny gave me a rather pitying look. 'Because he was thirsty, of course. Wouldn't you be after two fights? Can you see any water about? Anyway, it bonds me with my lads; it's all part of our special relationship.'

As silently as we'd come, we returned to the stile, Johnny gave a long, low whistle and, in a matter of seconds, the girls rejoined us. I was about to lean down to pat one of them, when Johnny sharply said, 'No. If you don't touch them, they won't touch you, but if you did I have them trained so they'd "nail" you.' I took him at his word, but must admit that I doubted it. They had such lovely friendly eyes and looked so loving when they gazed in adoration at their master. We walked in silence to within about fifty yards of the gate, when Johnny stopped and turned to me.

'Right, you go on, just in case anyone comes past.' He grinned wickedly, 'You don't want to be seen in the company of a poacher. You may not realise it, but you've watched something this morning not seen by many who aren't Romanies, so don't talk about it. I trusted you when I took you along. Don't let me down. Now you'd better be off. I'll see you again one day.'

That afternoon I again passed along by Cants Hill. The caravan had gone, the site was clean, no litter, even the ashes from the fire had been spread around on the grass. I kept Johnny's secret for many years and it wasn't until I met a retired gamekeeper, who was both very knowledgeable on country matters and loved to reminisce, that I learned that at one time, particularly before the First World War, a number of gypsies kept gamecocks for a similar purpose to Johnny's. My informant told me that he'd become very friendly with a gypsy family, real poachers, at a time when one of his dogs had a terrible skin infection and he was becoming desperate about curing it. He'd had it to the vet numerous times without success. One evening he had his dog with him, when he'd caught one of the gypsies poaching rabbits. The latter had noticed the state of the dog and told the keeper that if he would turn a blind eye to the rabbits, he'd cure the dog's skin. My keeper friend was so worried about his dog that he agreed. He told me, in some detail, how he'd gone back to the camp and been given a large pot of evil-smelling ointment, which he was to rub into the dog's skin every other day. The result, he said, was quite miraculous. Within weeks the dog was better.

From then on my friend called on the gypsies every time they camped in his area. Times were hard and he said nothing about rabbits and, indeed, a possible hare or two taken in roadside snares. He was interested in several gamecocks around the camp and, eventually, learned their purpose. Knowing if caught he was risking his job, he nonetheless invited his Romany friend to bring his gamecocks onto his beat and show their ability. This they did with the minimum of fuss. I must say that such a confession helped to ease my conscience, for, over many years, the memory of my excursion with Johnny had left me with the feeling that I had collaborated with the enemy!

My years at Reading were fruitful, as well as providing a very pleasant social life. There was a students' union, but I never remember it being very active. Other than organising a few debates and talks, its main job seemed to be arranging the dances in the assembly hall on Saturday evenings throughout the winter months. Admission was either 1s, maybe 1s 6d; whatever it was, it wasn't very much. These were no 'hops'. The men wore white tie and tails, dinner jackets were considered very infra dig and in bad taste. The girls were in long evening dresses, and many wore elbow-length gloves. The dances were great fun and we would adjourn, several times during the course of the evening, to The George, whose friendly landlord, Mr Porter, made students most welcome. It was virtually an unwritten law that the girls drank halves of mild, the boys halves of bitter. That way one could buy a round for four and get tuppence change out of a shilling. I remember taking a girl called Ruth to a dance. When, in due course, we went with another couple down to The George, without being asked she said hers was a gin and tonic – that cost more than a round of beer for four! It was noticeable that she was seldom partnered by the same man – her tastes were far too costly.

Discipline at the university was strict. One had to be properly dressed: no male student would have dared to go into a lecture without wearing a collar and tie, and the girls were always in skirts. Officially, we were supposed to wear gowns, but only freshmen did that and soon learned just to carry them, or leave them in hall. There was never a hint of a 'demonstration', such as students seem to regularly indulge in these days – we were all far too scared of the Censor of Discipline. Step out of line and it did not take a lot to be sent down. I remember once being called to his office. For the life of me I couldn't think what crime I could have committed, but, knees knocking, I presented myself at the time ordered. I was shown in, and there were no preliminaries; he immediately began to lambast me verbally for my irresponsible and dangerous behaviour the previous morning. It was several minutes before I was able to discover what I was supposed to have done. Apparently APH, my car, was said to have been seen going up Redlands Road, packed to overflowing, plus two men on each running board, all shouting and yelling and making gestures at other cars and pedestrians. Did I realise that, quite apart from being dangerous, I could be sent down immediately for such behaviour? At last the tirade ended.

Gulping, I asked, 'What time was this, sir?'

'I don't see what that's got to do with it. It was your car. However, my informant says it was precisely 11.30 a.m.'

I gave a sigh of relief. 'It wasn't me, sir. I was with Mr Black, my tutor, at that time.

The C. of D. glared at me. 'God help you if you're lying. Wait.'

He strode from the room and did not return for about ten minutes. 'Go. Luckily for you, Mr Black confirms your story, but it was your car. Don't let it happen again. Out.' He turned to his papers, no apology, not even a smile. I went – fast.

But how do you ensure something doesn't happen again when you can't take the ignition key out and there are no locks on the doors? I solved the problem, from then on, by taking the rotor arm out every time I parked at the university. I had no desire to meet the Censor of Discipline again!

It was July 1939. Final exams were over, leaving but a few rather nostalgic days before our year 'went down' for good. Parties and farewell functions were planned, in which my friends were involved, but I didn't join in many of them, at least not during the day. Haymaking was late. The weather in mid June had been nothing short of atrocious and I was urgently required to operate a haysweep. Much to my amazement and, equally, to my gratification, I was to be paid. I was to receive the princely sum of 1s per hour. I was in the money, as, if the weather remained hot and sunny, I could earn £3 for a sixty hour week, which was quite normal during haymaking and harvest. I asked if I'd get time and a quarter, like the men, if we worked overtime. I was quickly told not to push my luck.

There was much talk of war, but my friends and I at university did not truly believe Hitler would be so stupid, for, if he did, the combined power of the British Empire and France would crush the German army by Christmas. How wrong can one be? I was due to go out to South Africa in October to help care for a consignment of pedigree livestock being shipped out by Harry Hobson & Co. – an eagerly awaited trip – but it was not to be. Instead I was in camp in Berkshire with the Territorials, having joined, like a number of my friends, at the time of the Munich crisis. That autumn was the beginning of the end of an era and a way of life, which had changed very slowly over many decades and was soon destined to become only a wistful memory.